Good Food Made Simple

VEGETARIAN

Good Food Made Simple

VEGETARIAN

Over 140 delicious recipes, 500 colour photographs, step-by-step images and nutritional information

This edition published by Parragon Books Ltd in 2014
LOVE FOOD is an imprint of Parragon Books Ltd

Parragon Books Ltd
Chartist House
15–17 Trim Street
Bath BA1 1HA, UK
www.parragon.com/lovefood

ISBN 978-1-4723-5703-8

Printed in China

Additional design by Geoff Borin
New photography by Noel Murphy
New home economy by Sue Henderson
New recipes by Teresa Goldfinch
Introduction and notes by Sarah Bush
Edited by Fiona Biggs
Nutritional analysis by Fiona Hunter

Notes for the Reader
This book uses both metric and imperial measurements. Follow the same
units of measurement throughout; do not mix metric and imperial. All spoon
measurements are level: teaspoons are assumed to be 5 ml, and tablespoons
are assumed to be 15 ml. Unless otherwise stated, milk is assumed to be full fat,
eggs and individual vegetables are medium, and pepper is freshly ground black
pepper. Unless otherwise stated, all root vegetables should be peeled prior to
using.

Garnishes, decorations and serving suggestions are all optional and not
necessarily included in the recipe ingredients or method. Any optional
ingredients and seasoning to taste are not included in the nutritional analysis. The
times given are an approximate guide only. Preparation times differ according
to the techniques used by different people and the cooking times may also vary
from those given. Optional ingredients, variations or serving suggestions have not
been included in the time calculations.

Vegetarians should be aware that some of the ready-made ingredients used in the
recipes in this book may contain animal products. Always check the packaging
before use.

Contents

Vegetarian cooking

There are many misconceptions surrounding a vegetarian diet but, put simply, someone following this regime removes meat, fish and poultry from their meals and replaces them with vegetables, grains, pasta, beans, lentils, fresh fruit and nuts. Today, more and more people are considering replacing two or three main meals a week with a vegetarian alternative – others may have decided to convert totally.

Equally, almost all of us will know someone within our family circle or friends who is a vegetarian, so it is important to understand the basic principles when cooking for them.

Benefits of a vegetarian diet

You may be surprised, but the western diet used to consist mainly of cereals, pulses and vegetables because most people grew their own food or bought it locally and meat or poultry was considered a luxury only for special occasions. This high fibre, low-fat, low-sugar, low-salt diet was far healthier for us and illnesses that are common today were rare. The availability of mass-produced processed foods has made our lives easier, but is more of a concern for our health.

New inspirations

Today, being vegetarian is much easier than it was in the past. For a start there are so many more ingredients available in our supermarkets and speciality stores. Many other cultures, whose diets tend to revolve more around vegetables, are increasingly influential and we can draw on spicy seasonings from Asia, robust flavours from the Mediterranean and exciting grain dishes from Africa. Travelling to holiday destinations further afield has encouraged us to sample the unfamiliar and given us a desire to cook similar dishes back home. Restaurants are more aware of the changing trends of eating and include meatless choices on their menus which are enjoyed by vegetarians and non-vegetarians alike.

Explore your local ethnic food stores to find a range of exciting ingredients and spices.

Vegetarians and the environment

The range of fresh produce today is staggering and growers and producers are constantly tempting us with new foods. Growing our own vegetables, fruit and herbs is more popular and farmer's markets spring up regularly in towns all over the country. By shopping locally we support small businesses and help lessen our environmental impact. A supply of fresh, organically grown vegetables, fruit and salads are just on our door step – a boon to the vegetarian diet. Sometimes you pay a premium for this as harvesting is done on a smaller scale and often by hand rather than using large scale machinery, however if you're not buying more expensive meat and poultry items each week, the saving is transferred.

Vegetarians and vegans

When considering the pros and cons of changing your eating habits you should investigate the various approaches to vegetarian food. Some people consider themselves vegetarian yet they eat fish and others will eat chicken. Then there are those who follow the vegan diet and only eat foods of plant origin and therefore don't eat milk, butter, eggs, or even honey. Whichever route you choose, variety is the key to maintaining a balanced diet.

The recipes included in this book do not include any meat or fish products, but may contain dairy such as eggs, milk and cheese, so are not suitable for vegans, unless specified.

Maintaining a balanced diet

The vegetarian diet is not complicated or time consuming as is sometimes thought. Likewise it's not automatically healthy and requires the combination of different ingredients to achieve the right balance. Don't be worried about this aspect, just be aware of what your body needs to work efficiently and understand how you can ensure this.

Proteins

These are essential for healthy growth and repair of cells as well as protection against infection and building up resistance. The daily requirement for the body is quite small and there is no problem getting enough as long as you are following a varied vegetarian diet. The main sources are:

• Dairy - eggs, cheese, yogurt and milk.

• Cereals - rice, oats, corn, wheat and flour products, pasta, couscous, barley and rye.

• Pulses - dried beans including soya and soya bean products (such as tofu), chickpeas and lentils.

• Seeds and nuts - walnuts, brazil nuts, pecan nuts, almonds, cashew nuts, pine kernels, peanuts and peanut butter; pumpkin seeds, sunflower seeds, linseeds, sesame seeds and tahini paste.

Carbohydrates

The body needs carbohydrates for energy and they are found in starches and natural sugar. The easiest way to consume them is in the form of grains so foods using flour to make bread, cakes and biscuits should be included in the diet. Both pasta and potatoes are a good source too.

It's difficult to eat too many carbohydrates because they are the "filler" ingredients that we eat at most meals. They are not responsible for weight gain, as is often thought, as that tends to be due to excessive amounts of fat eaten with them.

Sugar

Refined sugar is an energy food and measured amounts found in jams, preserves and honey is the most straightforward way to include it in the diet. Too many of these calories, however, and the body will be unable to burn off the excess and they will be stored as body fat. Far better to enjoy the natural sugars that are packed into fresh fruit, which come with the added bonus of fibre and fill you up more quickly.

Fats

History shows us that fats and oils have been an essential ingredient in the human diet for centuries and they come from two sources - plants and animals. The only animal fat included in the vegetarian diet is that found in eggs or milk and products made from it such as cream, butter and cheese.

Other fats regularly used come from plants either in the form of oils or spreads and hard vegetable fats, such as margarine. There are many issues regarding the intake of fats, whether they are saturated (solid animal fats), unsaturated (olive oil) or polyunsaturated (vegetable oils) with many different opinions.

The healthiest is generally considered to be unsaturated fat and countries, such as those around the Mediterranean, that include this form of fat in the diet appear to have a lower incidence of heart disease.

Another consideration is that butter, which is a natural product, is preferable to using margarines and some oils that have been heavily processed. Whichever path you choose to take, it is generally accepted that a reduced intake of fat is the healthiest option.

Other essentials

To ensure a vegetarian diet is balanced and includes all the elements your body requires, you need to follow certain principles. Once you have become familiar with the best foods to eat in the right quantities everything else will fall into place. Plan your meals to include reasonable portions of grains and food made from them with plenty of fruit and vegetables. Eat moderate amounts of dairy, eggs, peas, beans, lentil and nuts and small portions of fats, sugar, tea, coffee and alcohol.

All these foods form part of a balanced diet so it shouldn't be necessary to take vitamin supplements, unless prescribed by your doctor.

Vitamins + minerals

While concentrating on other aspects of the vegetarian diet, sometimes the essential nutrients in the form of vitamins and minerals can be forgotten.

The body needs vitamins from the B group, iron and zinc to help process foods and allow the nervous system to function properly. They can be found in:

- wholegrain cereals
- breads and pasta
- nuts and seeds
- dried pulses
- potatoes
- fresh and dried fruit
- leafy green vegetables
- soya products
- yeast extract.

Combining foods

One other point to consider in the vegetarian diet is that by excluding certain foods which come from animal sources (meat, poultry and fish) you are excluding proteins that are known as "complete". When digested, these are used by the body to make essential proteins of its own.

Although cheese and eggs are also "complete" they can only be eaten by vegetarians in moderate quantities to avoid a fat overload and vegans do not have this option at all. It's necessary therefore to combine complementary proteins either in one meal or within a few hours. This is not as mysterious as it may appear and you probably do it already - just think hummus and pitta bread, pasta and cheese, muesli with nuts and seeds, baked beans on wholewheat toast.

Sourcing & substituting

Changing set eating habits will not happen overnight and don't worry if at first your menus aren't perfectly balanced. Each day will take you a step further to your chosen way of eating as you buy different ingredients and try out new recipes. Shop regularly for fresh vegetables and include them in as many meals as possible. Gradually change to wholefood products instead of the processed ones, choose reduced-fat versions of foods you usually buy and look more closely at lists of ingredients on packets to avoid high fat, salt or additives.

Start reading the small print on food labels to check what's included.

Hidden animal products

Animal products may be included in many ready-made foods.

For example:

- pastry may contain animal suet or lard

- cheese is often made with animal rennet as a coagulator

- sweets and desserts may include gelatine that comes from an animal source

- manufactured cakes will have eggs and dairy in them

- many bottled sauces contain anchovies

- wine can be made using animal products in the fining process.

Finding out more

If you are searching for more detailed information about what is contained in ready-made products, reputable sites on the internet offer a wealth of easily-accessed information and advice.

Storecupboard essentials

Start to build up a storecupboard of useful ingredients including dried pulses and wholewheat pasta. Keep a stock of different varieties of canned beans for quick meals, when you don't have time to soak them in advance. Have a selection of olive, seed and flavoured oils, dried spices and seasonings for the new recipes you will be discovering.

Freezing

Your freezer will be a good friend so take the time to cook double quantities of recipes that you can pack into containers to be used at a later date. There are hints about freezing many of the recipes in this book.

The everyday vegetarian

When you start out on the road to total or part-time vegetarianism, meal planning is going to be the first step. Your own favourite recipes will stand you in good stead by just replacing certain ingredients.

Some simple changes

• Make a Bolognese sauce with lentils replacing the meat (see page 174).

• A spicy Bean & Vegetable Chilli (see page 188) is a great alternative to a meat-based one.

• Home-made soups (see pages 68-88) can be made with vegetable stock and using grains or pulses to thicken.

• Bean Burgers (see page 202) will be winners with children.

• There's a huge range of delicious vegetarian toppings for pizza, including some more unusual sweet ones (see page 260).

Vegetarians and meat eaters

If you are catering for both vegetarians and non-vegetarians, it needn't be difficult and with a little thought about menus and planning, you will just need to make a few changes. Try to plan menus that everyone can eat, rather than cooking separate dishes. As long as a meal is balanced and varied, most people will be happy to eat vegetarian dishes – and may not even notice!

A vegetarian diet for children

When considering a vegetarian diet for children, exactly the same principles apply. Careful monitoring of their diet making sure they are not missing out on essential foods, will ensure that they are healthy, energetic and growing at the correct rate.

Few parents are able to raise children without worries and concerns over their eating patterns, but just be sure to include plenty of high vitality foods, ensure that as much as possible is fresh and unprocessed. Always have wholesome snacks available:

- precut fresh fruit

- small helpings of dried apricots, raisins and cranberries

- vegetable sticks

- rice cakes

- cheese cubes

- yogurts.

Offer water or diluted fruit juice rather than sweet fizzy drinks. You could also make your own ice lollies using fruit purée with little or no added sugar.

Involving children in helping to prepare and cook meals will encourage them to try new foods.

Above all, don't be daunted. Moving either wholly, or partly, towards a vegetarian diet is not difficult and will open the door to a tasty and healthy new approach to food and cooking that you and your friends and family will love.

Apple & Seed Muesli *18*

Oatmeal Crunch *20*

Honey & Rosemary Roast Plums *22*

Tropical Porridge *24*

Fresh Croissants *26*

Strawberry Breakfast Dip *28*

Eggs Florentine *30*

Muesli Pancake Stack with Honey *32*

French Toast Waffles *34*

Pancake Eggs Benedict *36*

Pancakes with Baked Mushrooms *38*

Mushroom Bruschetta *40*

Roast Pepper Ciabatta with Chopped Eggs & Olives *42*

Summer Fruit Croissants with Mascarpone *44*

Courgette Fritters with Eggs & Caramelized Onions *46*

Asparagus & Egg Pastries *48*

Cinnamon Swirls *50*

Apple Danish *52*

Yogurt with Blueberries, Honey & Nuts *54*

Muesli Muffins *56*

Melting Mozzarella Bagels *58*

Celery & Apple Revitalizer *60*

Red Pepper Booster *62*

Apricot Buzz *64*

Breakfast & Brunch

Apple & Seed Muesli

 SERVES 10

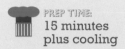 PREP TIME:
15 minutes
plus cooling

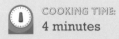 COOKING TIME:
4 minutes

nutritional information per serving	325 kcals, 12g fat, 1g sat fat, 16g total sugars, trace salt

Nutty and fruity, this is a great healthy start to the day. Serve with milk or pouring yogurt.

INGREDIENTS

75 g/2¾ oz sunflower seeds

50 g/1¾ oz pumpkin seeds

90 g/3¼ oz shelled hazelnuts, roughly chopped

125 g/4½ oz buckwheat flakes

125 g/4½ oz rice flakes

125 g/4½ oz millet flakes

115 g/4 oz no-soak dried apple, roughly chopped

115 g/4 oz dried stoned dates, roughly chopped

1. Heat a non-stick frying pan over a medium heat. Add the seeds and hazelnuts and lightly toast, shaking the pan frequently, for 4 minutes, or until golden brown. Transfer to a large bowl and leave to cool.

2. Add the flakes, apple and dates to the bowl and mix thoroughly until combined. Store the muesli in an airtight jar or container.

SOMETHING
DIFFERENT
For extra
sweetness and
crunch, try
topping with
slices of fresh
apple or pear.

Oatmeal Crunch

 SERVES 2   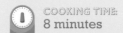 PREP TIME: 10 minutes    COOKING TIME: 8 minutes

nutritional information per serving	362 kcals, 17g fat, 2g sat fat, 7g total sugars, 0.5g salt

Make oatmeal more exciting with the addition of plump apricots, almonds and sunflower seeds. A great breakfast choice on chilly days.

INGREDIENTS

100 g/3½ oz rolled oats
450 ml/16 fl oz water
small pinch of salt
2 tbsp chopped ready-to-eat dried apricots
2 tbsp toasted flaked almonds
4 tsp sunflower seeds

1. Mix the oats with the water and salt in a non-stick saucepan and stir well. Bring to the boil over a medium–high heat, stirring occasionally, then reduce the heat and simmer, continuing to stir occasionally, for 5 minutes.

2. When the porridge is thick and creamy, spoon into two serving bowls and top with the apricots, almonds and sunflower seeds. Serve immediately.

HEALTHY HINT
If you prefer a creamier cereal, use half low-fat milk and half water.

Honey & Rosemary Roast Plums

 SERVES 4

 PREP TIME:
15 minutes
plus cooling

 COOKING TIME:
25–35 minutes

nutritional information per serving	316 kcals, 18g fat, 11g sat fat, 27g total sugars, 0.2g salt

These plums look pretty bathed in their ruby syrup.

INGREDIENTS

350 g/12 oz firm ripe red plums
3–4 fresh rosemary sprigs
6 tbsp clear honey
finely grated zest and juice of ½ orange
100 ml/3½ fl oz double cream
150 ml//5 fl oz Greek-style yogurt
60 g/2¼ oz crunchy muesli

1. Preheat the oven to 190°C/375°F/Gas Mark 5. Halve and stone the plums, then arrange them cut side up in an ovenproof dish large enough to hold them in a single layer. Bruise the rosemary sprigs with a rolling pin and push them among the fruit.

2. Mix together the honey, the orange juice and zest, then pour over the top of the plums. Cover the dish with foil and bake for 25–35 minutes in the preheated oven until the plums are tender. The exact cooking time will depend on the size and ripeness of the fruit. Leave to cool for 15 minutes, then remove the rosemary.

3. Meanwhile, whip the cream until it holds soft peaks. Add the yogurt and gently fold together.

4. To serve, divide the warm plums and their syrupy juices between four bowls. Add a large spoonful of the yogurt mixture to each bowl and sprinkle with the muesli.

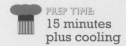

TO SERVE
To vary the
flavour, replace
the rosemary
with a split
vanilla pod or
cinnamon sticks.

Tropical Porridge

 SERVES 2    PREP TIME: 10 minutes    COOKING TIME: 8 minutes

nutritional information per serving	361 kcals, 10.5g fat, 2g sat fat, 24g total sugars, 0.5g salt

Try this recipe to turn ordinary porridge into a bowl of sunshine to brighten your day.

INGREDIENTS

100 g/3½ oz rolled oats

300 ml/10 fl oz hot water

pinch of salt

50 g/1¾ oz tropical fruit and nut mix

1 large or 2 small bananas

reduced-fat coconut milk, to serve

1. Put the oats into a non-stick saucepan and add the hot water and salt. Stir well and bring to the boil, then reduce the heat and simmer, stirring often, for 5 minutes, until the porridge is thick and fairly smooth.

2. When the porridge is nearly ready, stir in the tropical fruit and nut mix and cook for a further minute.

3. Spoon the porridge into two serving bowls. Peel the banana and slice it over the top. Serve immediately with reduced-fat coconut milk.

Fresh Croissants

 MAKES 12

 PREP TIME: 40 minutes plus rising

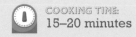 COOKING TIME: 15–20 minutes

nutritional information per croissant	372 kcals, 23g fat, 14g sat fat, 5g total sugars, 0.8g salt

You could start this recipe the night before. Make the dough and roll out the croissants, then brush with the glaze, cover with clingfilm and refrigerate overnight. The next morning, leave to prove for 30-45 minutes, then bake.

INGREDIENTS

500 g/1 lb 2 oz strong white bread flour, plus extra for rolling

40 g/1½ oz caster sugar

1 tsp salt

2 tsp easy-blend dried yeast

300 ml/10 fl oz milk, heated until just warm to the touch

300 g/10½ oz butter, softened, plus extra for greasing

1 egg, lightly beaten with 1 tbsp milk, for glazing

strawberry jam, to serve

1. Stir the dry ingredients into a large bowl, make a well in the centre and add the milk. Mix to a soft dough, adding more milk if too dry. Knead on a lightly floured work surface for 5–10 minutes, or until smooth and elastic. Leave to rise in a large greased bowl, covered, in a warm place until doubled in size. Meanwhile, flatten the butter with a rolling pin between two sheets of greaseproof paper to form a rectgle about 5 mm/¼ inch thick, then chill.

2. Knead the dough for 1 minute. Remove the butter from the refrigerator and leave to soften slightly. Roll out the dough on a well-floured work surface to 46 x 15 cm/18 x 6 inches. Place the butter in the centre, folding up the sides and squeezing the edges together gently. With the short end of the dough towards you, fold the top third down towards the centre, then fold the bottom third up. Rotate 90° clockwise so that the fold is to your left and the top flap towards your right. Roll out to a rectangle and fold again. If the butter feels soft, wrap the dough in clingfilm and chill. Repeat the rolling process twice more. Cut the dough in half. Roll out one half into a triangle 5 mm/¼ inch thick (keep the other half refrigerated). Use a cardboard triangular template, base 18 cm/7 inches and sides 20 cm/8 inches, to cut out six croissants. Repeat with the other half of the dough.

3. Preheat the oven to 200°C/400°F/Gas Mark 6. Brush the triangles lightly with the glaze. Roll into croissant shapes, starting at the base and tucking the point underneath to prevent unrolling while cooking. Brush again with the glaze. Place on an ungreased baking sheet and leave to double in size. Bake for 15–20 minutes until golden brown. Serve warm with jam.

1

1

2

Strawberry Breakfast Dip

 SERVES 4    PREP TIME: 10 minutes    COOKING TIME: No cooking

nutritional information per serving	166 kcals, 5g fat, 3g sat fat, 13g total sugars, 0.4g salt

You can make a stunning display of sliced fruits to serve with this delicious dip.

INGREDIENTS

100 g/3½ oz ripe strawberries, hulled and roughly chopped, plus extra to garnish

1 tbsp icing sugar

200 ml/7 fl oz natural fromage frais

1 tsp lemon juice

4 slices wholemeal bread

2 large pieces of fruit, such as a mango, nectarine or banana, cut into wedges

1. Process the strawberries with the icing sugar in a blender for a few seconds or mash with the sugar using a fork.

2. Combine the mixture with the fromage frais and lemon juice in a bowl. Spoon into a serving dish and chill, if you have time.

3. Toast the bread and cut into fingers. Arrange the fruit as dippers on a plate around the strawberry dip. Garnish the dip with half a fresh strawberry. Serve immediately.

1

2

3

SOMETHING
DIFFERENT
Serve small
shortbread
biscuits with
the dip for
a delicious
dessert.

Eggs Florentine

 SERVES 4    PREP TIME: 20 minutes    COOKING TIME: 35–40 minutes

nutritional information per serving	477 kcals, 39g fat, 16g sat fat, 7g total sugars, 1.1g salt

This classic dish is always a favourite for a special breakfast or a lazy weekend brunch.

INGREDIENTS

450 g/1 lb fresh spinach leaves, thoroughly washed

55 g/2 oz unsalted butter, plus extra for greasing

55 g/2 oz button mushrooms, sliced

55 g/2 oz pine kernels, toasted

6 spring onions, chopped

4 eggs

25 g/1 oz plain wholemeal flour

300 ml/10 fl oz milk, warmed

1 tsp prepared English mustard

85 g/3 oz mature vegetarian Cheddar cheese, grated

salt and pepper

1. Preheat the oven to 190°C/375°F/Gas Mark 5. Shake off any excess water from the spinach, put into a large saucepan over a medium heat with only the water clinging to the leaves and sprinkle with a little salt. Cover and cook for 2–3 minutes, or until wilted. Drain, pressing out any excess liquid, then chop and place in a greased ovenproof dish.

2. Heat 15 g/½ oz of the butter in a small saucepan over a medium heat, add the mushrooms and cook for 2 minutes, stirring frequently. Add the pine kernels and spring onions and cook for a further 2 minutes. Remove, from the heat, season to taste with salt and pepper and scatter over the spinach. Reserve and keep warm.

3. Meanwhile, fill a frying pan with cold water and bring to the boil, then reduce the heat to a gentle simmer. Carefully break an egg into a cup and slip it into the water. Add the remaining eggs and cook for 4–5 minutes, or until set. Carefully remove with a slotted spoon and arrange on top of the spinach mixture.

4. Melt the remaining butter in a saucepan and stir in the flour. Cook for 2 minutes, then remove from the heat and gradually stir in the milk. Return to the heat and cook, stirring constantly, until the mixture comes to the boil and has thickened. Stir in the mustard, then 55 g/ 2 oz of the cheese. Continue stirring until the cheese has melted. Add salt and pepper to taste, then pour over the eggs, completely covering them. Sprinkle with the remaining cheese.

5. Cook in the preheated oven for 20–25 minutes, or until piping hot and the top is golden brown and bubbling. Serve immediately.

Muesli Pancake Stack with Honey

 SERVES 4    PREP TIME: 15 minutes    COOKING TIME: 15 minutes

nutritional information per serving	385 kcals, 14g fat, 3.5g sat fat, 9g total sugars, 0.9g salt

This is a recipe that combines two breakfast favourites in one neat package. Using different muesli recipes, the variations are endless.

INGREDIENTS

150 g/5½ oz plain white flour
1½ tsp baking powder
pinch of salt
250 ml/9 fl oz milk
1 large egg
2 tbsp sunflower oil, plus extra for greasing
2 tbsp natural low-fat yogurt
140 g/5 oz muesli
clear honey, to serve

1. Sift the flour, baking powder and salt into a bowl. Add the milk, egg, oil and yogurt and whisk to a smooth batter. Stir in the muesli and leave to stand for 5 minutes.

2. Lightly grease a griddle pan or frying pan and heat over a medium heat. Spoon tablespoons of batter onto the pan and cook until bubbles appear on the surface.

3. Turn over with a palette knife and cook the other side until golden brown. Repeat this process using the remaining batter, while keeping the cooked pancakes warm.

4. Spoon honey over the pancakes and serve immediately.

SOMETHING
DIFFERENT
Try maple syrup
instead of honey
for a different
flavour.

French Toast Waffles

 SERVES 4   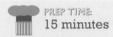 PREP TIME: 15 minutes   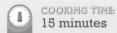 COOKING TIME: 15 minutes

nutritional information per serving	536 kcals, 19g fat, 11g sat fat, 20g total sugars, 1.4g salt

Similar to the traditional favourite "eggy bread", but when cooked in a waffle maker you create an altogether more impressive dish. Alternatively cook in a frying pan or in the oven on a baking tray.

INGREDIENTS

150 g/5½ oz plain white flour

1½ tsp baking powder

pinch of salt

1 tsp ground cinnamon

2 tbsp caster sugar

250 ml/9 fl oz milk

1 large egg

2 tbsp melted butter, plus extra to serve

sunflower oil, for greasing

8–10 slices brioche-type bread

demerara sugar, to serve

1. Sift the flour, baking powder, salt, cinnamon and sugar into a bowl. Add the milk, egg and butter and whisk to a smooth batter. Leave to stand for 5 minutes.

2. Lightly grease a waffle maker with the oil and heat until hot. Dip the slices of bread quickly into the batter, then place in the waffle maker and cook until golden brown. Repeat, using the remaining batter and bread, while keeping the cooked waffles warm.

3. Serve immediately, with melted butter and sugar.

BE PREPARED
Make waffles
in advance and
reheat in a
medium hot
oven when
required.

Pancake Eggs Benedict

 SERVES 4    PREP TIME: 15 minutes    COOKING TIME: 15 minutes

nutritional information per serving	350 kcals, 17g fat, 5g sat fat, 3g total sugars, 1.1g salt

This traditional dish always includes a generous helping of classic hollandaise sauce.

INGREDIENTS

150 g/5½ oz plain white flour
1½ tsp baking powder
pinch of salt
250 ml/9 fl oz milk
1 large egg
2 tbsp melted butter
sunflower oil, for greasing

topping
4 large eggs

hollandaise sauce
3 egg yolks
½ tsp English mustard
1 tbsp lemon juice
200 g/7 oz butter
salt and pepper

1. Sift the flour, baking powder and salt into a bowl. Add the milk, egg and butter and whisk to a smooth batter. Leave to stand for 5 minutes.

2. Lightly grease a griddle pan or frying pan with the oil and heat over a medium heat. Spoon tablespoons of batter onto the pan and cook until bubbles appear on the surface.

3. Turn over with a palette knife and cook the other side until golden brown. Repeat this process using the remaining batter, while keeping the cooked pancakes warm.

4. For the topping, bring a wide saucepan of water to the boil, then reduce the heat to a low simmer. Carefully break the eggs into the water and poach for about 3 minutes, until the whites are set but the yolks are still runny.

5. Meanwhile, make the sauce. Place the egg yolks, mustard and lemon juice in a blender and blend for a few seconds until smooth. Place the butter in a saucepan and heat until bubbling. With the motor running, gradually pour the butter into the egg yolks until the sauce is thickened and creamy. Season to taste with salt and pepper.

6. Place three overlapping pancakes on each plate with an egg on top. Spoon over the sauce, season to taste with salt and pepper and serve immediately.

Pancakes with Baked Mushrooms

 SERVES 6

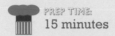 PREP TIME:
15 minutes

 COOKING TIME:
15 minutes

nutritional information per serving	295 kcals, 21g fat, 10g sat fat, 2.5g total sugars, 0.8g salt

The aroma from melted herby garlic butter on mushrooms will get the taste buds tingling.

INGREDIENTS

150 g/5½ oz plain white flour
1½ tsp baking powder
pinch of salt
250 ml/9 fl oz milk
1 large egg
2 tbsp melted butter
sunflower oil, for greasing

topping
55 g/2 oz butter
2 tbsp chopped fresh parsley
1 tbsp snipped chives
1 garlic clove, crushed
3 tbsp olive oil
12 field mushrooms
salt and pepper

1. For the topping, preheat the oven to 200°C/400°F/Gas Mark 6. Beat the butter until softened, stir in the parsley and chives and season to taste with salt and pepper.

2. Mix the garlic and oil together. Place the mushrooms on a baking sheet in a single layer, brush with the garlic oil and sprinkle with salt and pepper to taste. Bake in the oven for about 15 minutes, turning once, until tender.

3. Meanwhile, sift the flour, baking powder and salt into a bowl. Add the milk, egg and butter and whisk to a smooth batter. Leave to stand for 5 minutes.

4. Lightly grease a griddle pan or frying pan and heat over a medium heat. Spoon tablespoons of batter onto the pan and cook until bubbles appear on the surface.

5. Turn over with a palette knife and cook the other side until golden brown. Repeat this process using the remaining batter, while keeping the cooked pancakes warm.

6. Place a mushroom on each pancake, top with a spoonful of herb butter and serve immediately.

Mushroom Bruschetta

 SERVES 4 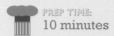 PREP TIME: 10 minutes  COOKING TIME: 10 minutes

nutritional information per serving	352 kcals, 11g fat, 1.5g sat fat, 3g total sugars, 1.6g salt

Mushrooms on toast have never looked or tasted so good!

INGREDIENTS

12 slices baguette, each 1 cm/
½ inch thick, or 2 individual
baguettes, cut lengthways

3 tbsp olive oil

2 garlic cloves, crushed

225 g/8 oz chestnut mushrooms,
sliced

225 g/8 oz mixed wild
mushrooms

2 tsp lemon juice

2 tbsp chopped fresh parsley

salt and pepper

1. Preheat the grill to medium–high. Place the slices of baguette on a ridged griddle pan and toast on both sides until golden. Reserve and keep warm.

2. Meanwhile, heat the oil in a frying pan. Add the garlic and cook gently for a few seconds, then add the chestnut mushrooms. Cook, stirring constantly, over a high heat for 3 minutes. Add the wild mushrooms and cook for a further 2 minutes. Stir in the lemon juice.

3. Season to taste with salt and pepper and stir in the chopped parsley.

4. Spoon the mushroom mixture onto the warm toast and serve immediately.

SOMETHING
DIFFERENT
Look out for
packs of mixed
mushrooms that
are ideal for
this recipe.

Roast Pepper Ciabatta with Chopped Eggs & Olives

 SERVES 4 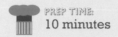 PREP TIME: 10 minutes  COOKING TIME: 15 minutes

nutritional information per serving	383 kcals, 15g fat, 2.5g sat fat , 8g total sugars, 1.4g salt

All the flavours of the Mediterranean in one big open sandwich and any leftovers are delicious eaten cold.

INGREDIENTS

2 eggs

55 g/2 oz pitted black olives, chopped

2 tbsp chopped fresh coriander leaves

1 large red pepper, deseeded and cut into thin strips

1 large green pepper, deseeded and cut into thin strips

1 large yellow pepper, deseeded and cut into thin strips

1 small red onion, finely chopped

1 garlic clove, finely chopped

1 tbsp chopped fresh oregano

2 tbsp olive oil

1 large ciabatta loaf

salt and pepper

lemon wedges, to serve

1. Place the eggs in a small saucepan, add hot water to cover and bring to the boil. Reduce the heat and simmer for 8 minutes. Drain, rinse under cold water and shell the eggs, then chop them and place in a bowl. Add the olives and coriander and season to taste with salt and pepper. Mix together and set aside.

2. Preheat the grill to high. Mix the red pepper, green pepper and yellow pepper strips with the onion, garlic, oregano and olive oil. Season to taste with salt and pepper.

3. Slice the ciabatta in half horizontally. Place cut sides down on the rack in a grill pan and toast the tops for about a minute, until crisp and lightly browned. Turn the bread. Arrange the pepper strips on the bread, covering it completely.

4. Grill the pepper-topped ciabatta for 4–5 minutes, until the peppers are softened and well browned in places. Top with the egg mixture and serve immediately with lemon wedges.

1

2

3

Summer Fruit Croissants with Mascarpone

 SERVES 4    PREP TIME: 40 minutes plus cooling   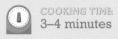 COOKING TIME: 3–4 minutes

nutritional information per serving	460 kcals, 33g fat, 20g sat fat, 11.5g total sugars, 0.7g salt

These croissants are quick to assemble, and everyone will think you've gone to lots more effort than you have!

INGREDIENTS

4 croissants

½ vanilla pod

175 g/6 oz vegetarian mascarpone cheese

1 tbsp icing sugar, plus extra for dusting

4 tbsp single cream

175 g/6 oz prepared soft fruit, such as strawberries, hulled and halved, blueberries and raspberries

1. Preheat the oven to 200°C/400°F/Gas Mark 6. Slice through the croissants horizontally, then reassemble them and place on a baking tray. Warm them in the preheated oven for 3–4 minutes.

2. Scrape the seeds from the vanilla pod into a small bowl. Add the mascarpone cheese, icing sugar and 2 tablespoons of the cream. Beat together until smooth then beat in the remaining cream.

3. Open up the warmed croissants. Divide the mascarpone mixture and the fruit between the bases, then replace the lids. Sift a little icing sugar over the top and serve immediately.

1

2

3

Courgette Fritters with Eggs & Caramelized Onions

 SERVES 4  PREP TIME: 40 minutes plus cooling  COOKING TIME: 45 minutes

nutritional information per serving	572 kcals, 33g fat, 6g sat fat, 14g total sugars, 0.8g salt

Make the caramelized onions in advance and store in the refrigerator for up to a week. If the batter mixture for the fritters seems too thick, stir in a little extra milk.

INGREDIENTS

2 tbsp extra virgin olive oil

5 red onions, sliced

1 tbsp soft brown sugar

200 g/7 oz self-raising flour

1 egg, lightly beaten, plus 4 eggs for poaching or frying

200 ml/7 fl oz milk

2 courgettes, grated

225 ml/8 fl oz sunflower oil

salt and pepper

1. Heat the olive oil in a large heavy-based saucepan over a medium heat, add the onions and cook for 5 minutes, or until softened. Stir in the sugar and reduce the heat, cover and cook for 30 minutes, or until the onions are deep brown in colour, stirring occasionally. Season to taste with salt and pepper and leave to cool.

2. To make the fritters, place the flour in a large bowl and make a well in the centre. Whisk the beaten egg and milk together and incorporate into the flour, using a wooden spoon to make a batter. Season to taste with salt and pepper and stir in the grated courgettes.

3. Heat the sunflower oil in a wide deep-sided pan and drop in tablespoons of the batter. Cook until golden brown on both sides, turning once. Drain on kitchen paper and keep warm.

4. Poach or fry the eggs, as you prefer. To serve, place three fritters on each individual plate, place an egg on top and spoon over some of the caramelized onions. Serve immediately.

Asparagus & Egg Pastries

 SERVES 4    PREP TIME: 15 minutes plus chilling   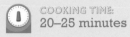 COOKING TIME: 20–25 minutes

nutritional information per serving	600 kcals, 37g fat, 16g sat fat, 6g total sugars, 1.7g salt

Spicy smoked paprika is the perfect complement to these baked eggs in puff pastry.

INGREDIENTS

500 g/1 lb 2 oz ready-made puff pastry

flour, for dusting

milk, for brushing

300 g/10½ oz slim asparagus spears

200 g/7 oz ready-made tomato pasta sauce

1 tsp hot smoked paprika

4 eggs

salt and pepper

1. Roll out the pastry on a lightly floured surface to a 35 x 20-cm/ 14 x 8-inch rectangle, then cut into four pieces to make four 20 x 9-cm/ 8 x 3½-inch rectangles. Line a baking tray with non-stick baking paper and place the pastry rectangles on the tray. Prick all over with a fork and brush lightly with milk. Chill for 20 minutes.

2. Snap the woody ends off the asparagus and discard. Bring a saucepan of lightly salted water to the boil, then add the asparagus, bring back to the boil and cook for 2–3 minutes until almost tender. Drain and refresh in cold water, then drain again.

3. Meanwhile, preheat the oven to 200°C/400°F/Gas Mark 6. Mix the tomato sauce and paprika together and divide between the pastry bases, spreading it out almost to the edges. Bake in the preheated oven for 10–12 minutes until the pastry is puffed around the edges and pale golden in colour.

4. Remove from the oven and arrange the asparagus on top, leaving space for the egg in the middle of each pastry. Crack one egg into a cup and slide into the space created in one of the pastries. Repeat with the remaining eggs, then return the pastries to the oven for 8 minutes, or until the eggs are just set. Season with salt and pepper and serve immediately.

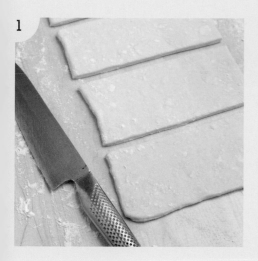

1

2

4

Cinnamon Swirls

 MAKES 12

 PREP TIME:
20 minutes
plus rising

 COOKING TIME:
20–30 minutes

nutritional information per pastry	165 kcals, 7g fat, 4g sat fat, 9g total sugars, 0.3g salt

*The delicious smell of baking cinnamon flavoured dough
will bring everyone into the kitchen for a taste.*

INGREDIENTS

25 g/1 oz butter, cut into small
pieces, plus extra for greasing
225 g/8 oz strong white flour
½ tsp salt
1 sachet easy-blend dried yeast
1 egg, lightly beaten
125 ml/4 fl oz lukewarm milk
2 tbsp maple syrup, for glazing

filling
55 g/2 oz butter, softened
2 tsp ground cinnamon
50 g/1¾ oz soft light brown sugar
50 g/1¾ oz currants

1. Grease a baking sheet and a bowl. Sift the flour and salt into a separate mixing bowl and stir in the yeast. Rub in the chopped butter with your fingertips until the mixture resembles breadcrumbs. Add the egg and milk and mix to form a dough.

2. Form the dough into a ball, place in the greased bowl, cover and leave to stand in a warm place for about 40 minutes, or until doubled in volume. Punch down the dough lightly for 1 minute, then roll out to a rectangle measuring 30 x 23 cm/12 x 9 inches.

3. For the filling, cream together the softened butter, cinnamon and sugar until light and fluffy. Spread the filling over the dough, leaving a 2.5-cm/1-inch border. Sprinkle the currants evenly over the top. Roll up the dough from one of the long edges and press down to seal.

4. Preheat the oven to 190°C/375°F/Gas Mark 5. Cut the roll into 12 slices and place them, cut side down, on the prepared baking sheet. Cover and leave to stand for 30 minutes.

5. Bake in the preheated oven for 20–30 minutes, or until the swirls are well risen. Brush with maple syrup and leave to cool slightly before serving.

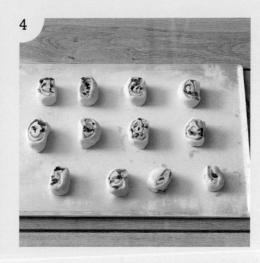

Apple Danish

 MAKES 16    PREP TIME: 20 minutes plus chilling    COOKING TIME: 25–30 minutes

nutritional information per pastry	180 kcals, 10g fat, 6g sat fat, 7.5g total sugars, 0.3g salt

This is the classic recipe that originated in Scandinavia and has been happily adopted by the rest of the world.

INGREDIENTS

275 g/9¾ oz strong white flour, plus extra, sifted, for dusting

175 g/6 oz butter, well chilled, plus extra for greasing

½ tsp salt

1 sachet easy-blend dried yeast

2 tbsp caster sugar, plus extra for sprinkling

1 egg

1 tsp vanilla extract

6 tbsp lukewarm water

milk, for glazing

filling

2 cooking apples, peeled, cored and chopped

grated rind of 1 lemon

3 tbsp sugar

1. Place the flour in a bowl and rub in 25 g/1 oz of the butter. Set aside. Dust the remaining butter with flour, grate coarsely into a bowl and chill. Stir the salt, yeast and sugar into the flour mixture.

2. In another bowl, beat the egg with the vanilla extract and water, add to the flour mixture and mix to form a dough. Knead for 10 minutes on a floured surface, then chill for 10 minutes.

3. Roll out the dough to a 30 x 20-cm/12 x 8-inch rectangle. Mark widthways into thirds and fold. Press the edges with a rolling pin and roll out to the same size as the original rectangle. Sprinkle the grated butter evenly over the top two-thirds. Fold up the bottom third and fold down the top third. Press the edges, wrap in clingfilm and chill for 30 minutes. Repeat four times, chilling well each time. Chill overnight.

4. Mix the filling ingredients together. Preheat the oven to 200°C/400°F/Gas Mark 6. Grease two baking sheets. Roll out the dough into a 40-cm/16-inch square and cut into 16 squares. Pile some filling in the centre of each, reserving any juice. Brush the edges of the squares with milk and bring the corners together in the centre. Place on the prepared baking sheets and chill for 15 minutes. Brush with the reserved juice and sprinkle with caster sugar.

5. Bake in the preheated oven for 10 minutes, reduce the temperature to 180°C/350°F/Gas Mark 4 and bake for a further 10–15 minutes, until browned. Gently remove from the baking sheets and serve warm.

Yogurt with Blueberries, Honey & Nuts

 SERVES 4  PREP TIME: 10 minutes plus cooling  COOKING TIME: 5 minutes

nutritional information per serving	215 kcals, 11g fat, 2g sat fat, 18g total sugars, trace salt

Greek yogurt served topped with fresh berries, honey and nuts is a quick and delicious breakfast treat.

INGREDIENTS

3 tbsp clear honey

85 g/3 oz mixed unsalted nuts

8 tbsp reduced-fat Greek-style yogurt

200 g/7 oz fresh blueberries

1. Heat the honey in a small saucepan over medium heat. Add the nuts and stir until they are well coated. Remove from the heat and leave to cool slightly.

2. Divide the yogurt among four serving bowls, then spoon over the nut mixture and the blueberries and serve immediately.

COOK'S NOTE
Serve as an easy and fresh-tasting dessert. If blueberries are not available use any berry in season.

Muesli Muffins

nutritional information
per muffin

234 kcals, 9g fat, 1.5g sat fat, 14g total sugars, 0.5g salt

Everyone loves muffins and these are no exception.
Great for lunch boxes too.

INGREDIENTS

140 g/5 oz plain flour
1 tbsp baking powder
280 g/10 oz unsweetened muesli
115 g/4 oz soft light brown sugar
2 eggs
250 ml/9 fl oz buttermilk
6 tbsp sunflower oil

1. Preheat the oven to 200°C/400°F/Gas Mark 6. Place 12 paper cases in a muffin tin.

2. Sift together the flour and baking powder into a large bowl. Stir in the muesli and sugar.

3. Place the eggs in a large jug or bowl and beat lightly, then beat in the buttermilk and oil. Make a well in the centre of the dry ingredients and pour in the beaten liquid ingredients. Stir gently until just combined; do not over-mix. Spoon the mixture into the paper cases.

4. Bake in the preheated oven for about 20 minutes, or until well risen, golden brown and firm to the touch. Leave to cool in the tin for 5 minutes, then serve warm or transfer to a wire rack to cool.

FREEZING TIP
Freeze in
zippered plastic
bags for up
to 1 month.
Defrost at
room temperature.

Melting Mozzarella Bagels

 SERVES 4   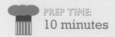 PREP TIME: 10 minutes    COOKING TIME: 20 minutes

nutritional information **per serving**   419 kcals, 19g fat, 7g sat fat, 7g total sugars, 1.5g salt

A really filling start to the day, the quantities can easily be increased to feed a larger crowd. Swap the basil leaves for rocket if you prefer.

INGREDIENTS

½ aubergine, thinly sliced

3–4 tbsp olive oil

4 onion bagels or plain bagels

175 g/6 oz vegetarian mozzarella cheese, sliced

1 beef tomato, thinly sliced

salt and pepper

6–8 fresh basil leaves, torn in half if large, to serve

1. Preheat a griddle pan until smoking. Brush the aubergine slices with a little of the oil, place on the pan and cook for 2 minutes on each side until tender and lightly charred.

2. Preheat the oven to 190°C/375°F/Gas Mark 5. Split the bagels in half and drizzle the cut sides with the remaining oil. Divide the cheese slices between the bagel bases and arrange the slices of tomato and aubergine on top. Season with salt and pepper and replace the bagel tops.

3. Place on a baking tray and bake in the preheated oven for 15 minutes until the cheese has melted and the bagels are beginning to toast around the edges. Add a few fresh basil leaves to each bagel and serve immediately.

BE PREPARED
Get ahead by assembling the bagels and placing them in the refrigerator the night before, ready to pop in the oven at the last minute.

Celery & Apple Revitalizer

 SERVES 2    PREP TIME: 5 minutes    COOKING TIME: No cooking

nutritional information per serving	225 kcals, 12g fat, 7g sat fat, 20g total sugars, 0.5g salt

A milkshake that does you good! Celery and apple are the perfect combination in this drink that is great on hot summer days. Serve in tall glasses with strips of celery to decorate.

INGREDIENTS

115 g/4 oz celery, chopped

1 eating apple, peeled, cored and diced

600 ml/1 pint milk

pinch of sugar (optional)

salt (optional)

strips of celery, for decorating

1. Place the celery, apple and milk in a blender and process until thoroughly combined.

2. Stir in the sugar and some salt, if using. Pour into chilled glasses, decorate with strips of celery and serve.

1

2

2

HEALTHY HINT
For a thicker
drink use half
milk and half
liquid yogurt.

Red Pepper Booster

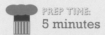 SERVES 2    PREP TIME:
5 minutes   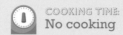 COOKING TIME:
No cooking

nutritional information
per serving   113 kcals, 0.9g fat, 0g sat fat, 22g total sugars, 0.9g salt

Pour yourself a glass of goodness. This is the perfect choice for a healthier drink option and will look really inviting served in a jug with ice cubes.

INGREDIENTS

250 ml/9 fl oz carrot juice
250 ml/9 fl oz tomato juice
2 large red peppers, deseeded
and roughly chopped
1 tbsp lemon juice
pepper
lemon slices, to garnish

1. Pour the carrot juice and tomato juice into a food processor or blender and process gently until combined.

2. Add the red peppers and lemon juice. Season with plenty of pepper and process until smooth. Pour the mixture into glasses, garnish with lemon slices and serve.

SOMETHING
DIFFERENT
Have Tabasco
sauce available
for adding
some heat.

Apricot Buzz

 SERVES 2    PREP TIME: 5 minutes   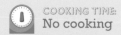 COOKING TIME: No cooking

nutritional information per serving	52 kcals, 0.2g fat, 0g sat fat, 11g total sugars, trace salt

When apricots are ripe and bursting with flavour, this Asian inspired "mocktail" will really go down well. Serve with ice on a warm summer morning.

INGREDIENTS

6 apricots
1 orange
1 fresh lemon grass stalk
2-cm/¾-inch piece fresh ginger, peeled

1. Halve and stone the apricots. Peel the orange, leaving some of the white pith. Cut the lemon grass into chunks.

2. Place the apricots, orange, lemon grass and ginger in a juicer and juice all the ingredients together. Pour the mixture into glasses, add ice and serve.

1

2

2

Indian Potato & Pea Soup *68*

Spicy Courgette Soup with Rice & Lime *70*

Pea & Herb Soup with Basil Oil *72*

Vegetable & Corn Chowder *74*

Roast Squash Soup with Cheese Toasties *76*

Thai Vermicelli Soup *78*

Spicy Lentil Soup *80*

Minty Pea & Bean Soup *82*

White Bean Soup *84*

Vichyssoise *86*

French Onion Soup *88*

Mini Roast Vegetable Skewers *90*

Aubergine Pâté *92*

Blue Cheese & Herb Pâté *94*

Couscous with Roast Cherry Tomatoes & Pine Kernels *96*

Vegetable Pakoras *98*

Roasted Vegetable & Feta Cheese Wraps *100*

Hot & Sour Courgettes *102*

Spicy Avocado Dip *104*

Mushrooms with Garlic & Spring Onions *106*

Feta, Lemon & Herb Dip *108*

Roast Fennel with Cherry Tomatoes & Rosemary *110*

Braised Peas with Lettuce & Tarragon *112*

Green Leaf & Herb Chutney with Olives *114*

Soups, Starters & Sides

Indian Potato & Pea Soup

 SERVES 4    PREP TIME: 10 minutes    COOKING TIME: 30 minutes

nutritional information per serving	150 kcals, 7g fat, 1g sat fat, 4g total sugars, 0.5g salt

This easy recipe makes a really tasty soup with just the right amount of spice.

INGREDIENTS

2 tbsp vegetable oil

225 g/8 oz floury potatoes, diced

1 large onion, chopped

2 garlic cloves, crushed

1 tsp garam masala

1 tsp ground coriander

1 tsp ground cumin

850 ml/1½ pints vegetable stock

1 fresh red chilli, deseeded and chopped

100 g/3½ oz frozen peas

4 tbsp natural yogurt

salt and pepper

chopped fresh coriander, to garnish

1. Heat the vegetable oil in a large saucepan. Add the potatoes, onion and garlic and sauté over a low heat, stirring constantly, for about 5 minutes. Add the garam masala, ground coriander and cumin and cook, stirring constantly, for 1 minute.

2. Stir in the vegetable stock and red chilli and bring the mixture to the boil. Reduce the heat, cover the pan and simmer for 20 minutes, until the potatoes begin to break down. Add the peas and cook for a further 5 minutes. Stir in the yogurt and season to taste with salt and pepper. Ladle into warmed bowls, garnish with chopped coriander and serve immediately.

GOES WELL WITH
Serve warm naan
bread or crispy
poppadoms as an
accompaniment.

Spicy Courgette Soup with Rice & Lime

 SERVES 4    PREP TIME: 10 minutes   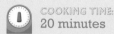 COOKING TIME: 20 minutes

nutritional information per serving	195 kcals, 6g fat, 0.7g sat fat, 0.8g total sugars, 1g salt

A squeeze of lime added to this light, fresh tasting soup makes all the difference.

INGREDIENTS

2 tbsp vegetable oil

4 garlic cloves, thinly sliced

1–2 tbsp mild red chilli powder

¼ –½ tsp ground cumin

1.5 litres/2¾ pints vegetable stock

2 courgettes cut into bite-sized chunks

4 tbsp long-grain rice

salt and pepper

fresh oregano sprigs, to garnish

lime wedges, to serve

1. Heat the oil in a heavy-based saucepan. Add the garlic and cook for 2 minutes, or until softened. Add the chilli powder and cumin and cook over a medium–low heat for 1 minute.

2. Stir in the stock, courgettes and rice, then cook over a medium–high heat for 10 minutes, or until the courgettes are just tender and the rice is cooked through. Season to taste with salt and pepper.

3. Ladle into warmed bowls, garnish with oregano sprigs and serve immediately with lime wedges.

SOMETHING
DIFFERENT
Use a combination
of green and
yellow courgettes
for extra colour.

Pea & Herb Soup with Basil Oil

 SERVES 4

 PREP TIME: 12 minutes plus chilling

 COOKING TIME: 15–20 minutes

nutritional information **per serving**   277 kcals, 22g fat, 8g sat fat, 4g total sugars, 0.2g salt

This elegant soup is delicious hot or chilled.

INGREDIENTS

30 g/1 oz butter
6 spring onions, chopped
1 celery stick, finely chopped
375 g/13 oz frozen peas or fresh shelled peas
700 ml/1¼ pints vegetable stock
2 tbsp chopped fresh dill
1 tbsp snipped fresh chives
35 g/1¼ oz rocket leaves
2 tbsp crème fraîche
salt and pepper
bread sticks, to serve

basil oil
1 x 30-g/1-oz bunch of basil
200 ml/7 fl oz olive oil

1. Melt the butter in a saucepan over a medium heat. Add the spring onions and celery, cover and cook for 5 minutes until soft. Add the peas and stock, bring to the boil and simmer for 10 minutes. Remove from the heat. Cover and leave to cool for 20 minutes.

2. To make the basil oil, remove the stems from the basil and discard. Place the leaves in a food processor with half the oil and blend to a purée. Add the remaining oil and blend again. Transfer to a small bowl.

3. Add the dill, chives and rocket to the soup. Blend with a hand-held blender until smooth. Stir in the crème fraîche. If serving warm, heat through gently without boiling, then season to taste.

4. Ladle into four warmed bowls and drizzle with the basil oil. Serve immediately, with bread sticks on the side. If serving chilled, leave to cool completely, then chill in the refrigerator for at least 1 hour before checking the seasoning and serving.

COOK'S NOTE
Any leftover
basil oil can
be stored in
the refrigerator
for 3-4 days
and used for
drizzling over
salads or ciabatta
or tossing with
pasta.

Vegetable & Corn Chowder

 SERVES 4   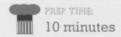 PREP TIME: 10 minutes   COOKING TIME: 25–30 minutes

nutritional information per serving | 363 kcals, 16g fat, 8g sat fat, 14g total sugars, 0.8g salt

Chowder is traditionally from New England in the United States and is another name for a thick, hearty soup.

INGREDIENTS

1 tbsp vegetable oil

1 red onion, diced

1 red pepper, deseeded and diced

3 garlic cloves, crushed

300 g/10½ oz potatoes, diced

2 tbsp plain flour

600 ml/1 pint milk

300 ml/10 fl oz vegetable stock

50 g/1¾ oz broccoli florets

300 g/10½ oz canned sweetcorn, drained

75 g/2¾ oz vegetarian Cheddar cheese, grated

salt and pepper

1. Heat the oil in a large saucepan. Add the onion, red pepper, garlic and potatoes and sauté over a low heat, stirring frequently, for 2–3 minutes.

2. Stir in the flour and cook, stirring, for 30 seconds. Gradually stir in the milk and stock.

3. Add the broccoli and sweetcorn. Bring the mixture to the boil, stirring constantly, then reduce the heat and simmer for about 20 minutes, or until all the vegetables are tender.

4. Stir in 50 g/1¾ oz of the cheese until it melts. Season to taste and ladle into warmed bowls. Garnish with the remaining cheese and serve immediately.

GOES WELL WITH
Serve with crusty sourdough or wholemeal bread for a satisfying lunch.

Roast Squash Soup with Cheese Toasties

 SERVES 4    PREP TIME: 20 minutes   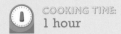 COOKING TIME: 1 hour

nutritional information per serving	548 kcals, 26g fat, 13g sat fat, 16g total sugars, 1.4g salt

A comforting, velvety textured soup that's perfect for freezing.

INGREDIENTS

1 kg/2 lb 4 oz butternut squash, cut into small chunks

2 onions, cut into wedges

2 tbsp olive oil

2 garlic cloves, crushed

3–4 fresh thyme sprigs, leaves removed

1 litre/1¾ pints vegetable stock

150 ml/5 fl oz crème fraîche

salt and pepper

snipped fresh chives, to garnish

toasties

1 baguette, thinly sliced diagonally

40 g/1½ oz vegetarian hard cheese, grated

1. Preheat the oven to 190°C/375°F/Gas Mark 5. Place the squash, onions, oil, garlic and thyme leaves in a roasting tin. Toss together and spread out in a single layer. Roast for 50–60 minutes, stirring occasionally, until the vegetables are tender and caramelized in places.

2. Transfer the vegetables to a saucepan. Add half the stock and purée with a hand-held blender until smooth. Alternatively, blend in a food processor, then transfer to a saucepan. Stir in the remaining stock and crème fraîche. Season to taste with salt and pepper, and heat through gently.

3. To make the toasties, preheat the grill to high. Toast the sliced baguette under the preheated grill for 1–2 minutes on each side until pale golden in colour. Sprinkle with the cheese and return to the grill for a further 30–40 seconds until melted and bubbling.

4. Ladle the soup into four warmed bowls and sprinkle with chives to garnish. Serve immediately with the cheese toasties on the side.

Thai Vermicelli Soup

 SERVES 4    PREP TIME: 25 minutes   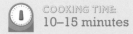 COOKING TIME: 10–15 minutes

nutritional information per serving	177 kcals, 5.5g fat, 0.4g sat fat, 2g total sugars, 0.9g salt

Try this light, spicy soup at the beginning of a Thai inspired meal – it will awaken the taste buds. Shiitake mushrooms really give an authentic flavour and are available in larger supermarkets or Asian stores.

INGREDIENTS

15 g/½ oz dried shiitake mushrooms
1.2 litres/2 pints vegetable stock
1 tbsp groundnut oil
4 spring onions, sliced
115 g/4 oz baby corn, sliced
2 garlic cloves, crushed
2 fresh kaffir lime leaves, chopped
2 tbsp red curry paste
85 g/3 oz rice vermicelli noodles
1 tbsp light soy sauce
2 tbsp chopped fresh coriander, to garnish

1. Place the mushrooms in a bowl, cover with the vegetable stock and leave to soak for 20 minutes.

2. Heat the groundnut oil in a saucepan over a medium heat. Add the spring onions, baby corn, garlic and kaffir lime leaves. Fry for 3 minutes to soften.

3. Add the red curry paste, soaked mushrooms and their soaking liquid. Bring to the boil and simmer for 5 minutes, stirring occasionally.

4. Add the noodles and soy sauce to the red curry mixture in the pan. Return the pan to the boil and simmer for a further 4 minutes until the noodles are just cooked. Ladle into warmed bowls, garnish with the chopped coriander and serve immediately.

1

2

3

SOMETHING DIFFERENT
Use corncobs instead
of baby corn. Stand
the cobs upright on
a board and with a
sharp knife cut down
from the top to remove
all the kernels from
one or two cobs.

Spicy Lentil Soup

 SERVES 4    PREP TIME: 5 minutes    COOKING TIME: 35–40 minutes

nutritional information per serving	235 kcals, 6g fat, 0.8g sat fat, 2g total sugars, trace salt

Just the recipe when you want a simple soup packed with great flavours.

INGREDIENTS

1 litre/1¾ pints water

250 g/9 oz toor dahl or chana dahl

1 tsp paprika

½ tsp chilli powder

½ tsp ground turmeric

2 tbsp ghee or vegetable oil

1 fresh green chilli, deseeded and finely chopped

1 tsp cumin seeds

3 curry leaves, roughly torn

1 tsp sugar

salt

1 tsp garam masala, to garnish

1. Bring the water to the boil in a large, heavy-based saucepan. Add the dahl, cover and simmer, stirring occasionally, for 25 minutes.

2. Stir in the paprika, chilli powder and turmeric, re-cover and cook for a further 10 minutes, or until the dahl is tender.

3. Meanwhile, heat the ghee in a small frying pan. Add the chilli, cumin seeds and curry leaves and cook, stirring constantly, for 1 minute.

4. Add the spice mixture to the dahl. Stir in the sugar and season to taste with salt. Ladle into warmed bowls, garnish with garam masala and serve immediately.

FREEZING TIP
If you find a fresh supply of curry leaves it's worth freezing them in a zippered bag to use when you fancy making a dish like this.

Minty Pea & Bean Soup

 SERVES 4    PREP TIME: 10 minutes   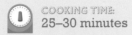 COOKING TIME: 25–30 minutes

nutritional information
per serving   176 kcals, 6g fat, 0.8g sat fat, 3.5g total sugars, 0.7g salt

A delicious summery soup, especially if you are lucky enough to have peas in your garden.

INGREDIENTS

1½ tbsp olive oil

1 bunch spring onions, chopped

1 large celery stick, chopped

1 garlic clove, crushed

1 floury potato, about 150 g/5½ oz, peeled and diced

1.2 litres/2 pints vegetable stock

1 bay leaf

150 g/5½ oz peas

400 g/14 oz canned flageolet beans, drained and rinsed

salt and pepper

finely shredded fresh mint, to garnish

mixed-grain bread rolls, to serve

1. Heat the oil in a large saucepan over a medium–high heat. Add the spring onions, celery and garlic and cook, stirring, for about 3 minutes, or until soft. Add the potato and stir for a further minute.

2. Add the stock and bay leaf. Season to taste with salt and pepper and bring to the boil, stirring. Reduce the heat to low, cover the pan and simmer for 20 minutes, or until the potatoes are tender.

3. Add the peas and beans and return the soup to the boil. Reduce the heat, re-cover the pan and continue to simmer until the peas are tender.

4. Remove and discard the bay leaf, then tip the soup into a food processor or blender and process until smooth. Place a metal sieve over the rinsed-out pan and use a wooden spoon to push the soup through the sieve.

5. Reheat gently. Ladle the soup into warmed bowls, garnish with mint and serve immediately with bread rolls.

1

3
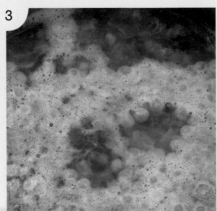

4

White Bean Soup

 SERVES 4

 PREP TIME:
10 minutes
plus soaking

 COOKING TIME:
2 hours 20 minutes

nutritional information
per serving 384 kcals, 18g fat, 2.5g sat fat, 1.5g total sugars, trace salt

A traditional Italian country soup from Tuscany that's worth starting the day before as the flavours will improve.

INGREDIENTS

175 g/6 oz dried cannellini beans, soaked in cold water to cover overnight

1.5 litres/2¾ pints vegetable stock

115 g/4 oz dried corallini, conchigliette piccole, or other soup pasta

6 tbsp olive oil

2 garlic cloves, finely chopped

4 tbsp chopped fresh flat-leaf parsley

salt and pepper

fresh crusty bread, to serve

1. Drain the soaked beans and place them in a large, heavy-based saucepan. Add the stock and bring to the boil. Partially cover the pan, then reduce the heat and simmer for 2 hours, or until tender.

2. Transfer about half the beans and a little of the stock to a food processor or blender and process to a smooth purée. Return the purée to the pan and stir well to mix. Return to the boil.

3. Add the pasta, return to the boil and cook for 10 minutes, or until tender.

4. Meanwhile, heat 4 tablespoons of the olive oil in a small saucepan. Add the garlic and cook over a low heat, stirring frequently, for 4–5 minutes, or until golden. Stir the garlic mixture into the soup and add the parsley. Season with salt and pepper and ladle into warmed bowls. Drizzle with the remaining olive oil and serve immediately with crusty bread.

1

2

3

GOES WELL WITH
Green salad leaves tossed with balsamic dressing and topped with shavings of cheese.

Vichyssoise

 SERVES 6

 PREP TIME: 40 minutes plus chilling

 COOKING TIME: 35 minutes

nutritional information per serving	309 kcals, 22g fat, 14g sat fat, 8g total sugars, 0.3g salt

A really delicious chilled soup for summer entertaining but equally good served hot when the weather is chilly.

INGREDIENTS

450 g/1 lb leeks, white parts only
450 g/1 lb potatoes
55 g/2 oz butter
1.2 litres/2 pints water
600 ml/1 pint milk
300 ml/10 fl oz soured cream, plus extra to garnish
salt and pepper
2 tbsp snipped fresh chives, to garnish

1. Thinly slice the leeks. Peel and dice the potatoes. Melt the butter in a large, heavy-based saucepan over a very low heat. Add the leeks, cover and cook, stirring occasionally, for 10 minutes.

2. Stir in the potatoes and cook over a medium heat, stirring frequently, for 2 minutes. Pour in the water and add a pinch of salt. Bring to the boil, then reduce the heat and simmer for 15–20 minutes until the potatoes are tender. Remove from the heat and leave to cool slightly. Transfer to a blender or food processor and process into a purée. Push the mixture through a sieve into a clean saucepan with a wooden spoon, then stir in the milk. Season to taste with salt and pepper and stir in half the soured cream.

3. Reheat the soup, then push through a sieve into a bowl. Stir in the remaining cream, cover with clingfilm and leave to cool. Chill in the refrigerator for 4–8 hours. Serve in chilled bowls, with swirls of soured cream and chives to garnish.

FREEZING TIP

Freeze for up to 3 months. Defrost fully and stir well before serving cold or reheat gently.

French Onion Soup

 SERVES 6    PREP TIME: 30 minutes    COOKING TIME: 1½ hours

nutritional information per serving	432 kcals, 24g fat, 11g sat fat, 8g total sugars, 1.4g salt

Traditionally a soup served throughout the night to workers at the famous Les Halles market in Paris.

INGREDIENTS

675 g/1 lb 8 oz onions

3 tbsp olive oil

4 garlic cloves, 3 chopped and 1 peeled but kept whole

1 tsp sugar

2 tsp chopped fresh thyme, plus extra sprigs to garnish

2 tbsp plain flour

125 ml/4 fl oz dry white wine

2 litres/3½ pints vegetable stock

6 slices French bread

300 g/10½ oz vegetarian Gruyère cheese, grated

1. Thinly slice the onions. Heat the oil in a large, heavy-based saucepan over a medium–low heat, add the onions and cook, stirring occasionally, for 10 minutes, or until they are just beginning to brown. Stir in the chopped garlic, sugar and chopped thyme, then reduce the heat and cook, stirring occasionally, for 30 minutes, or until the onions are golden brown.

2. Sprinkle in the flour and cook, stirring constantly, for 1–2 minutes. Stir in the wine. Gradually stir in the stock and bring to the boil, skimming off any foam that rises to the surface, then reduce the heat and simmer for 45 minutes. Meanwhile, preheat the grill to medium–high. Toast the bread on both sides under the grill, then rub the toast with the whole garlic clove.

3. Ladle the soup into six flameproof bowls set on a baking tray. Float a piece of toast in each bowl and divide the grated cheese between them. Place under the grill for 2–3 minutes, or until the cheese has just melted. Garnish with thyme sprigs and serve at once.

Mini Roast Vegetable Skewers

 SERVES 4    PREP TIME: 10 minutes    COOKING TIME: 25–30 minutes

nutritional information per serving	135 kcals, 8g fat, 2g sat fat, 10g total sugars, 0.2g salt

Roasting vegetables in the oven brings out their natural sweetness and the pieces stay in neat shapes too.

INGREDIENTS

1 red pepper, deseeded
1 yellow pepper, deseeded
1 large courgette
1 aubergine
2 tbsp olive oil
3 garlic cloves, crushed
salt and pepper

dip
2 tbsp chopped fresh dill
2 tbsp chopped fresh mint
250 ml/9 fl oz natural yogurt

1. Preheat the oven to 200°C/400°F/Gas Mark 6. Cut the vegetables into 2 cm/¾ inch chunks. Place in a roasting tin large enough to hold them in a single layer.

2. Mix the olive oil and garlic together and drizzle over the top. Season well with salt and pepper then toss together. Roast for 25–30 minutes until tender and lightly charred.

3. Meanwhile, stir the dill and mint into the yogurt. Spoon into four serving bowls.

4. When the vegetables are cool enough to handle, divide them between 12 cocktail sticks. Serve warm or cold with the bowls of dip on the side.

BE PREPARED
Cut the vegetables into chunks in advance and marinate for several hours or overnight.

Aubergine Pâté

 SERVES 6 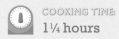 PREP TIME: 10 minutes plus cooling  COOKING TIME: 1¼ hours

nutritional information per serving	73 kcals, 7.5g fat, 1g sat fat, 1g total sugars, trace salt

Also known as Poor Man's Caviar because the humble aubergine when prepared this way tastes so delicious!

INGREDIENTS

2 large aubergines

4 tbsp extra virgin olive oil

2 garlic cloves, very finely chopped

4 tbsp lemon juice

salt and pepper

2 tbsp roughly chopped fresh flat-leaf parsley, to garnish

6 crisp breads, to serve

1. Preheat the oven to 180°C/350°F/Gas Mark 4. Score the skins of the aubergines with the point of a sharp knife, without piercing the flesh, and place them on a baking sheet. Bake for 1¼ hours, or until soft.

2. Remove the aubergines from the oven and leave until cool enough to handle. Cut them in half and, using a spoon, scoop out the flesh into a bowl. Mash the flesh thoroughly.

3. Gradually beat in the olive oil then stir in the garlic and lemon juice. Season to taste with salt and pepper. Cover with clingfilm and store in the refrigerator until required. Sprinkle with the parsley and serve with crisp breads.

1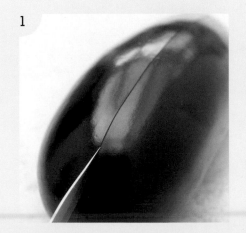

2

3

Blue Cheese & Herb Pâté

 SERVES 4  PREP TIME: 15 minutes plus chilling 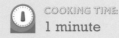 COOKING TIME: 1 minute

nutritional information per serving | 509 kcals, 42g fat, 25g sat fat, 5g total sugars, 1.3g salt

If you're stuck for something to serve as a starter or pack for a posh picnic, this pâté is ideal.

INGREDIENTS

150 g/5½ oz vegetarian low-fat soft cheese

350 g/12 oz fromage frais

115 g/4 oz vegetarian blue cheese, crumbled

55 g/2 oz dried cranberries, finely chopped

5 tbsp chopped fresh herbs, such as parsley, chives, dill and tarragon

85 g/3 oz butter

2 tbsp chopped walnuts

granary toast or bread sticks, to serve

1. Beat the soft cheese to soften, then gradually beat in the fromage frais until smooth. Add the blue cheese, cranberries and herbs. Stir together. Spoon the mixture into four 150-ml/5-fl oz ramekins or small dishes and carefully smooth the tops.

2. Clarify the butter by gently heating it in a small saucepan until melted. Skim any foam off the surface and discard. Carefully pour the clear yellow top layer into a small jug, leaving the milky liquid in the pan. The yellow layer is the clarified butter. Discard the liquid left in the pan.

3. Pour a little of the clarified butter over the top of each pâté and sprinkle with the walnuts. Chill for at least 30 minutes until firm. Serve with granary toast.

1

1

3

SOMETHING DIFFERENT

The blue cheese can be replaced with tangy vegetarian goat's cheese if you prefer.

Couscous with Roast Cherry Tomatoes & Pine Kernels

 SERVES 4

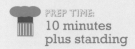 PREP TIME:
10 minutes
plus standing

 COOKING TIME:
8 minutes

nutritional information
per serving — 210 kcals, 14g fat, 1.5g sat fat, 2.5g total sugars, trace salt

This looks really pretty made with mixed red and yellow cherry tomatoes.

INGREDIENTS

300 g/10½ oz cherry tomatoes
3 tbsp olive oil
125 g/4½ oz couscous
200 ml/7 fl oz boiling water
30 g/1 oz pine kernels, toasted
5 tbsp roughly chopped
fresh mint
finely grated zest of 1 lemon
½ tbsp lemon juice
salt and pepper

1. Preheat the oven to 220°C/425°F/Gas Mark 7. Place the tomatoes and 1 tablespoon of the oil in a ovenproof dish. Toss together, then roast for 7–8 minutes in the preheated oven until the tomatoes are soft and the skins have burst. Leave to stand for 5 minutes.

2. Put the couscous in a heatproof bowl. Pour over the boiling water, cover and leave to stand for 8–10 minutes until soft and the liquid is absorbed. Fluff up with a fork.

3. Add the tomatoes and their juices, the pine kernels, mint, lemon zest, lemon juice and the remaining oil to the couscous. Season with salt and pepper, then gently toss together. Serve warm or cold.

GOES WELL WITH

This goes well
with a crisp
green salad and
some vegetarian
feta cheese or
chargrilled
halloumi.

Vegetable Pakoras

 SERVES 4

 PREP TIME: 20 minutes

 COOKING TIME: 15 minutes

nutritional information per serving	236 kcals, 12g fat, 1.5g sat fat, 4g total sugars, 0.6g salt

Serve these crunchy vegetable fritters piping hot as a snack or part of an Indian inspired meal.

INGREDIENTS

6 tbsp gram flour
½ tsp salt
1 tsp chilli powder
1 tsp baking powder
1½ tsp white cumin seeds
1 tsp pomegranate seeds
300 ml/10 fl oz water
¼ bunch of fresh coriander, finely chopped, plus extra sprigs to garnish

vegetables of your choice
cauliflower, cut into small florets; onions, cut into rings; potatoes, sliced; aubergines, sliced; or fresh spinach leaves
vegetable oil, for deep-frying

1. Sift the gram flour into a large bowl. Add the salt, chilli powder, baking powder, cumin and pomegranate seeds and blend together well. Pour in the water and beat well to form a smooth batter. Add the chopped coriander and mix well, then set aside.

2. Dip the prepared vegetables into the batter, carefully shaking off any excess.

3. Heat enough oil for deep-frying in a wok, deep-fat fryer or a large, heavy-based saucepan until it reaches 180°C/350°F, or until a cube of bread browns in 30 seconds. Using tongs, place the battered vegetables in the oil and deep-fry, in batches, turning once.

4. Repeat this process until all of the batter has been used up. Transfer the battered vegetables to crumpled kitchen paper and drain thoroughly. Garnish with coriander sprigs and serve immediately.

COOK'S NOTE
As the pakoras cook, transfer them to a wire rack placed on a baking tray in a medium-hot oven to keep warm until all the batches are cooked.

Roasted Vegetable & Feta Cheese Wraps

 SERVES 4

 PREP TIME:
10 minutes
plus cooling

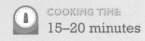 COOKING TIME:
15–20 minutes

nutritional information
per serving

373 kcals, 20g fat, 7g sat fat, 5g total sugars, 2.4g salt

Wraps are so convenient and this is one of the many delicious combinations you can fill them with.

INGREDIENTS

1 red onion, cut into eighths

1 red pepper, deseeded and cut into eighths

1 small aubergine, cut into eighths

1 courgette, cut into eighths

4 tbsp extra virgin olive oil

1 garlic clove, crushed

100 g/3½ oz vegetarian feta cheese, crumbled

small bunch of fresh mint, shredded

4 x 25-cm/10-inch sun-dried tomato wraps

salt and pepper

1. Preheat the oven to 220°C/425°F/Gas Mark 7. Mix all of the vegetables, olive oil, garlic and salt and pepper together and place in the oven in a non-stick oven tray. Roast for 15–20 minutes or until golden and cooked through.

2. Remove from the oven and leave to cool. Once cool, mix in the feta and mint.

3. Preheat a non-stick pan or grill pan until almost smoking, then cook the wraps one at a time on both sides for 10 seconds. This will add some colour and also soften the wraps.

4. Divide the vegetable and feta mixture between the wraps, placing it along the middle of each wrap. Roll up the wrap, cut them in half and serve immediately.

1

2

4

SOMETHING
DIFFERENT
You could spread
a spicy salsa
or creamy
hummus on the
wrap before
filling with the
other ingredients.

Hot & Sour Courgettes

 SERVES 4

 PREP TIME:
30 minutes

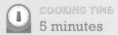 COOKING TIME:
5 minutes

nutritional information per serving	86 kcals, 7g fat, 1.5g sat fat, 4g total sugars, 1.9g salt

In a traditional Sichuan style this is just one more way to serve the humble courgette.

INGREDIENTS

2 large courgettes, thinly sliced

1 tsp salt

2 tbsp groundnut oil

1 tsp Sichuan peppercorns, crushed

½–1 red chilli, deseeded and sliced into thin strips

1 large garlic clove, thinly sliced

½ tsp finely chopped fresh ginger

1 tbsp rice vinegar

1 tbsp light soy sauce

2 tsp sugar

1 spring onion, green part included, thinly sliced

a few drops of sesame oil and 1 tsp sesame seeds, to garnish

1. Put the courgette slices in a large colander and toss with the salt. Cover with a plate and put a weight on top. Leave to drain for 20 minutes. Rinse off the salt and spread out the slices on kitchen paper to dry.

2. Preheat a wok over a high heat and add the groundnut oil. Add the Sichuan peppercorns, chilli, garlic and ginger. Fry for about 20 seconds until the garlic is just beginning to colour.

3. Add the courgette slices and toss in the oil. Add the rice vinegar, soy sauce and sugar, and stir-fry for 2 minutes. Add the spring onion and fry for 30 seconds. Garnish with the sesame oil and seeds, and serve immediately.

1

2

3

Spicy Avocado Dip

 SERVES 4    PREP TIME:
10 minutes   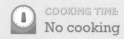 COOKING TIME:
No cooking

nutritional information per serving	192 kcals, 19g fat, 4g sat fat, 1g total sugars, trace salt

When choosing avocados for this great tasting dip, go for the crinkly skinned ones which have a better flavour. Check the ripeness too - they should just give slightly when pressed gently with your thumb.

INGREDIENTS

2 large avocados
juice of 1–2 limes
2 large garlic cloves, crushed
1 tsp mild chilli powder,
or to taste, plus extra to garnish
salt and pepper

1. Cut the avocados in half. Remove the stones and skin and discard.

2. Place the avocado flesh in a food processor with the juice of 1 or 2 limes, according to taste. Add the garlic and chilli powder and process until smooth.

3. Season to taste with salt and pepper. Transfer to a serving bowl, garnish with chilli powder and serve.

1

2

2

SOMETHING DIFFERENT

Add some diced, deseeded tomatoes or cucumber to the mixture for added crunch.

Mushrooms with Garlic & Spring Onions

 SERVES 4 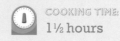 PREP TIME: 10 minutes plus cooling  COOKING TIME: 1½ hours

nutritional information per serving	80 kcals, 6g fat, 1g sat fat, 2g total sugars, trace salt

There may seem to be a huge amount of garlic in this recipe but don't worry, when you roast whole bulbs in the oven in this way they become milder, sweeter and deliciously caramelized.

INGREDIENTS

2 garlic bulbs

2 tbsp olive oil

350 g/12 oz assorted mushrooms, such as chestnut, open-cap and chanterelles, halved if large

1 tbsp chopped fresh parsley

8 spring onions, cut into 2.5-cm/1-inch lengths

salt and pepper

1. Preheat the oven to 180°C/350°F/Gas Mark 4. Slice off the tops of the garlic bulbs and press down to loosen the cloves. Place them in an ovenproof dish and season with salt and pepper to taste. Drizzle 2 teaspoons of the oil over the bulbs and roast for 30 minutes. Remove from the oven and drizzle with 1 teaspoon of the remaining oil. Return to the oven and roast for an additional 45 minutes. Remove the garlic from the oven and, when cool enough to handle, peel the cloves.

2. Tip the oil from the dish into a heavy-based frying pan. Add the remaining oil and heat. Add the mushrooms and cook over a medium heat, stirring frequently, for 4 minutes.

3. Add the garlic cloves, parsley and spring onions and cook, stirring frequently, for 5 minutes. Season with salt and pepper to taste and serve immediately.

GOES WELL WITH
Serve on toasted
ciabatta bread or
with scrambled
eggs.

Feta, Lemon & Herb Dip

 SERVES 5

 PREP TIME: 5 minutes plus chilling

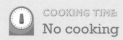 COOKING TIME: No cooking

nutritional information per serving	117 kcals, 10g fat, 5g sat fat, 0.3g total sugars, 1g salt

This quickly made dip is also lovely served as an accompaniment to vegetable kebabs and jacket potatoes.

INGREDIENTS

150 g/5½ oz vegetarian low fat soft cheese

3 tbsp water

1 tbsp olive oil

100 g/3½ oz vegetarian feta cheese, crumbled

1 large lemon

3 tbsp roughly chopped fresh mint

3 tbsp roughly chopped fresh dill

pepper

a selection of vegetable crudités, to serve

1. Place the soft cheese, water and oil in a food processor and process until smooth. Add the feta cheese and process briefly to combine, but make sure there are still some small lumps remaining. Transfer to a bowl.

2. Pare the zest from the lemon using a zester. Stir the zest into the dip with the mint and dill. Season with pepper. Cover and chill for at least 30 minutes to develop the flavours. Serve with a selection of vegetable crudités for dipping.

GET AHEAD
The dip and crudités can be prepared a day ahead and kept in the refrigerator.

Roast Fennel with Cherry Tomatoes & Rosemary

 SERVES 4

 PREP TIME: 5 minutes

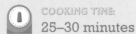 COOKING TIME: 25–30 minutes

nutritional information per serving	100 kcals, 7.5g fat, 1g sat fat, 3g total sugars, 0.2g salt

A lovely side dish for the summer months when these vegetables are at their cheapest and best.

INGREDIENTS

4 fennel bulbs, cut into slim wedges

2 tbsp olive oil

6 tbsp dry white wine

2 garlic cloves, crushed

2 tsp chopped fresh rosemary

200 g/7 oz cherry tomatoes

16 stoned black olives

2 tbsp chopped fresh parsley

salt and pepper

1. Preheat the oven to 200°C/400°F/Gas Mark 6. Place the fennel in a roasting tin large enough to hold it in a single layer. Mix the oil, 2 tablespoons of the wine, the garlic and rosemary together. Pour the mixture over the fennel, season with salt and pepper and toss together.

2. Roast in the preheated oven for 15–20 minutes until almost tender and lightly browned. Scatter the tomatoes and olives over the fennel. Pour over the remaining wine, then return to the oven for 8–10 minutes until the tomatoes are soft and the skins have burst. Toss with the parsley and serve warm or cold.

GOES WELL WITH
To turn this side dish into a light meal, toss with couscous and toasted pine kernels or with pasta and grated vegetarian Parmesan-style cheese.

Green Leaf & Herb Chutney with Olives

 SERVES 4    PREP TIME: 10 minutes plus cooling   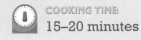 COOKING TIME: 15–20 minutes

nutritional information per serving	95 kcals, 9.5g fat, 1.5g sat fat, 1g total sugars, 0.3g salt

With a vibrant green colour and zingy combination of herbs and spices, this is perfect spread on bread but equally good as a dip or accompaniment to main course dishes.

INGREDIENTS

225 g/8 oz fresh baby spinach leaves

handful of celery leaves

3 tbsp olive oil

2–3 garlic cloves, crushed

1 tsp cumin seeds

6–8 black olives, stoned and finely chopped

1 large bunch of fresh flat-leaf parsley leaves, finely chopped

1 large bunch of fresh coriander leaves, finely chopped

1 tsp Spanish smoked paprika

juice of ½ lemon

salt and pepper

toasted flat bread or crusty bread and black olives, to serve

1. Place the spinach and celery leaves in a steamer and steam until tender. Refresh the leaves under cold running water, drain well and squeeze out the excess water. Place the steamed leaves on a wooden chopping board and chop to a pulp.

2. Heat 2 tablespoons of the oil in a heavy-based casserole. Add the garlic and cumin seeds, then cook over a medium heat for 1–2 minutes, stirring, until they emit a nutty aroma. Stir in the olives with the parsley and coriander and add the paprika.

3. Toss in the pulped spinach and celery and cook over a low heat, stirring occasionally, for 10 minutes until the mixture is smooth and compact. Season with salt and pepper to taste and leave to cool.

4. Tip the mixture into a bowl and bind with the remaining oil and the lemon juice. Serve with toasted flat bread or crusty bread and olives.

1

1

3

Crunchy Thai-style Salad *118*

Avocado Salad with Lime Dressing *120*

Couscous Salad with Roasted Butternut Squash *122*

Greek Salad Crostini *124*

Grilled Halloumi Kebabs on Fennel & White Bean Salad *126*

Sweet & Sour Noodles *128*

Spicy Chickpeas *130*

Thai Tofu Cakes with Chilli Dip *132*

Spicy Pak Choi with Sesame Sauce *134*

Mexican Rice *136*

Stir-fried Broccoli *138*

Caramelized Apple & Blue Cheese Salad *140*

Vegetable & Hazelnut Loaf *142*

Pepper & Basil Pots *144*

Creamy Mushroom Pancakes *146*

Potato & Chive Pancakes *148*

Crispy Crêpes with Ratatouille *150*

Aubergine, Pepper & Basil Crêpe Rolls *152*

Feta & Spinach Tartlets *154*

Lattice Flan *156*

Glazed Beetroot & Egg Sourdough Toasties *158*

Tomato Tarte Tatin *160*

Risotto with Asparagus & Walnuts *162*

Spicy Polenta with Poached Eggs *164*

Salads & Light Meals

Crunchy Thai-style Salad

 SERVES 4

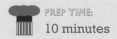 PREP TIME:
10 minutes

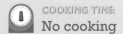 COOKING TIME:
No cooking

nutritional information per serving	74 kcals, 3g fat, 0.5g sat fat, 8g total sugars, 1.4g salt

Crispy, crunchy and full of flavour, this salad uses fragrant firm mangoes.

INGREDIENTS

1 slightly under ripe mango

5 Romaine or Cos lettuce leaves, torn into pieces

100 g/3½ oz beansprouts

handful of fresh coriander leaves

25 g/1 oz roasted unsalted peanuts, crushed

dressing

juice of 1 lime

2 tbsp light soy sauce

1 tsp soft light brown sugar

1 shallot, very thinly sliced

1 garlic clove, finely chopped

1 red bird's eye chilli, very thinly sliced

1 tbsp chopped fresh mint

1. To make the dressing, mix the lime juice, soy sauce and sugar together in a bowl then stir in the shallot, garlic, chilli and mint.

2. Peel the mango using a sharp knife or potato peeler. Slice the flesh from either side and around the stone. Thinly slice or shred the flesh.

3. Place the torn lettuce, beansprouts, coriander leaves and mango in a serving bowl. Gently toss together. Spoon the dressing over the top, scatter with the peanuts and serve immediately.

Avocado Salad with Lime Dressing

 SERVES 4    PREP TIME: 10 minutes   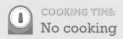 COOKING TIME: No cooking

nutritional information per serving	290 kcals, 28g fat, 5g sat fat, 4.5g total sugars, 0.1g salt

A perfect choice for a light lunch, this salad is as delightful to look at as it is to eat.

INGREDIENTS

60 g/2¼ oz mixed red and green lettuce leaves

60 g/2¼ oz wild rocket

4 spring onions, finely diced

5 tomatoes, sliced

25 g/1 oz walnuts, toasted and chopped

2 avocados

1 tbsp lemon juice

lime dressing
1 tbsp lime juice

1 tsp French mustard

1 tbsp sour cream

1 tbsp chopped fresh parsley or coriander

3 tbsp extra virgin olive oil

pinch of sugar

salt and pepper

1. Wash and drain the lettuce and rocket, if necessary. Shred all the leaves and arrange in the bottom of a large salad bowl. Add the spring onions, tomatoes and walnuts.

2. Stone, peel and thinly slice or dice the avocados. Brush with the lemon juice to prevent discoloration, then transfer to the salad bowl. Gently mix together.

3. To make the dressing, put all the dressing ingredients in a screw-top jar and shake well. Drizzle over the salad and serve immediately.

Greek Salad Crostini

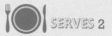 SERVES 2   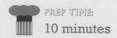 PREP TIME: 10 minutes    COOKING TIME: 5 minutes

nutritional information per serving	655 kcals, 50g fat, 18g sat fat, 11g total sugars, 4.4g salt

Crisp toasted country bread topped with a salad that packs in the flavours.

INGREDIENTS

1 garlic clove, crushed

4 tbsp olive oil

2 thick slices from a large, seeded loaf

200 g/7 oz vegetarian feta cheese, diced

pepper

¼ cucumber, finely diced

25 g/1 oz black olives, sliced

4 plum tomatoes, diced

½ small onion, chopped

2 sprigs fresh mint leaves, shredded

2 sprigs fresh oregano leaves, chopped

¼ tsp sugar

1 heart Little Gem lettuce, finely shredded

½ tsp toasted sesame seeds

2 tsp pine kernels (optional)

1. Preheat the grill to a medium–high setting. Mix the garlic and olive oil in a bowl large enough to mix all the salad ingredients.

2. Place the bread on the rack in the grill pan. Brush lightly with the garlic oil and toast well away from the heat for 2–3 minutes, until crisp and golden. Turn the bread and brush lightly with more oil, then toast again.

3. Add the feta cheese to the garlic oil remaining in the bowl and season with pepper (the cheese and olives usually provide enough salt). Mix in the cucumber, olives, tomatoes, onion, mint and oregano. Sprinkle with the sugar and mix well. Finally, lightly mix in the lettuce.

4. Transfer the crostini to plates and spoon the salad and its juices over them. Sprinkle with the sesame seeds and pine kernels (if using) and serve immediately, while the crostini are hot and crisp.

2

3

3

Sweet & Sour Noodles

 SERVES 4

 PREP TIME:
10 minutes

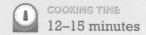 COOKING TIME:
12–15 minutes

nutritional information per serving	254 kcals, 6g fat, 1.5g sat fat, 14g total sugars, 2.3g salt

Increase the protein content by adding some toasted cashew nuts, cubed firm tofu, cooked black beans or toasted mixed seeds with the noodles at step 3.

INGREDIENTS

140 g/5 oz dried medium egg noodles

2 tsp sunflower oil

1 large red pepper, deseeded and thinly sliced

150 g/5½ oz beansprouts

5 spring onions, thinly sliced

3 tbsp Chinese cooking wine or dry sherry

salt

sauce

3 tbsp light soy sauce

2 tbsp clear honey

2 tbsp tomato purée

2 tsp cornflour

2 tsp sesame oil

100 ml/3½ fl oz vegetable stock

1. Bring a large saucepan of lightly salted water to the boil. Add the noodles, bring back to the boil and cook for 4 minutes until tender but still firm to the bite. Alternatively, cook according to the packet instructions. Drain.

2. To make the sauce, put the soy sauce, honey, tomato purée, cornflour and sesame oil into a small bowl and mix together until smooth, then stir in the stock.

3. Heat the sunflower oil in a wok or large, heavy-based frying pan. Add the red pepper and stir-fry for 4 minutes until soft. Add the beansprouts and stir-fry for 1 minute. Add the noodles and spring onions, then pour the wine and sauce over the top. Toss together over the heat for 1–2 minutes until the sauce is bubbling and thickened and the noodles have heated through. Serve immediately.

Spicy Chickpeas

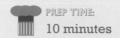 SERVES 4

 PREP TIME: 10 minutes

 COOKING TIME: 10–12 minutes

nutritional information per serving	190 kcals, 2.2g fat, 0.2g sat fat, 10g total sugars, 0.4g salt

This traditional Indian dish goes really well with plain boiled rice and a cucumber raita.

INGREDIENTS

400 g/14 oz canned chickpeas, drained
2 potatoes, diced
2 tbsp tamarind paste
6 tbsp water
1 tsp chilli powder
2 tsp sugar
1 onion, chopped
salt

to garnish
1 tomato, sliced
2 fresh green chillies, chopped
2–3 tbsp chopped fresh coriander

1. Place the drained chickpeas in a large bowl.

2. Place the potatoes in a saucepan of water and boil for 10-12 minutes or until cooked through. Drain and set aside.

3. Mix the tamarind paste and water together in a small bowl.

4. Add the chilli powder, sugar and 1 teaspoon of salt to the tamarind paste mixture and mix together. Pour the mixture over the chickpeas.

5. Add the onion and the diced potatoes, and stir to mix.

6. Transfer to a serving bowl and garnish with tomato, chillies and chopped coriander. Serve immediately.

2

5

5

Thai Tofu Cakes with Chilli Dip

 SERVES 4

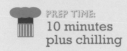 PREP TIME:
10 minutes
plus chilling

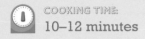 COOKING TIME:
10–12 minutes

nutritional information per serving	226 kcals, 10g fat, 1.5g sat fat, 5g total sugars, 0.7g salt

Similar to a fish cake, this Thai favourite would also make a great starter or snack with drinks.

INGREDIENTS

300 g/10½ oz firm tofu, drained weight, coarsely grated

1 lemon grass stalk, finely chopped

2 garlic cloves, chopped

2.5-cm/1-inch piece fresh ginger, grated

2 kaffir lime leaves, finely chopped (optional)

2 shallots, finely chopped

2 fresh red chillies, deseeded and finely chopped

4 tbsp chopped fresh coriander

90 g/3¼ oz plain flour, plus extra for dusting

½ tsp salt

corn oil, for cooking

chilli dip
3 tbsp white distilled vinegar

2 spring onions, finely sliced

1 tbsp caster sugar

2 fresh chillies, chopped

2 tbsp chopped fresh coriander

pinch of salt

1. To make the chilli dip, mix all the ingredients together in a small serving bowl and set aside.

2. Mix the tofu with the lemon grass, garlic, ginger, lime leaves, if using, shallots, chillies and coriander in a mixing bowl. Stir in the flour and salt to make a coarse, sticky paste. Cover and chill in the refrigerator for 1 hour to let the mixture firm up slightly.

3. Form the mixture into eight large walnut-sized balls and, using floured hands, flatten into circles. Heat enough oil to cover the bottom of a large, heavy-based frying pan over medium heat. Cook the cakes in two batches, turning halfway through, for 4–6 minutes, or until golden brown. Drain on kitchen paper and serve warm with the chilli dip.

Spicy Pak Choi with Sesame Sauce

 SERVES 4    PREP TIME: 10 minutes    COOKING TIME: 8–10 minutes

nutritional information per serving	163 kcals, 14g fat, 2g sat fat, 4.5g total sugars, 1.7g salt

Pak Choi is also known as Bok Choi and is a member of the cabbage family. Choose the smaller more tender ones with perky leaves and unblemished stalks.

INGREDIENTS

2 tsp groundnut or vegetable oil
1 red chilli, deseeded and thinly sliced
1 garlic clove, thinly sliced
5 small pak choi, quartered
100 ml/3½ fl oz vegetable stock

sauce
25 g/1 oz sesame seeds
2 tbsp dark soy sauce
2 tsp soft light brown sugar
1 garlic clove, crushed
3 tbsp sesame oil

1. For the sesame sauce, toast the sesame seeds in a dry frying pan set over a medium heat, stirring until lightly browned. Remove from the heat and cool slightly. Transfer to a pestle and mortar. Add the soy sauce, sugar and crushed garlic and pound to a coarse paste. Stir in the sesame oil.

2. Heat the groundnut oil in a wok or large frying pan. Add the chilli and sliced garlic and stir-fry for 20–30 seconds. Add the pak choi and stir-fry for 5 minutes, adding the stock a little at a time to prevent sticking.

3. Transfer the pak choi to a warmed dish, drizzle the sesame sauce over the top and serve immediately.

COOK'S NOTE
This sesame sauce recipe is a great standby to keep in the fridge as it's excellent poured over most steamed vegetables.

Mexican Rice

 SERVES 4

 PREP TIME:
10 minutes

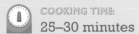 COOKING TIME:
25–30 minutes

nutritional information per serving	210 kcals, 1g fat, 0.1g sat fat, 4g total sugars, trace salt

Colourful tomato flavoured rice is great for serving to the family with a wide selection of main dishes.

INGREDIENTS

1 onion, chopped

400 g/14 oz plum tomatoes, peeled, deseeded and chopped

250 ml/9 fl oz vegetable stock

200 g/7 oz long-grain rice

salt and pepper

1. Put the onion and tomatoes in a food processor and process to a smooth purée. Scrape the purée into a saucepan, pour in the stock and bring to the boil over a medium heat, stirring occasionally.

2. Add the rice and stir once, then reduce the heat, cover and simmer for 20–25 minutes until all the liquid has been absorbed and the rice is tender. Season to taste with salt and pepper and serve immediately.

SOMETHING
DIFFERENT
Serve with your
favourite chilli
sauce if you like
some heat.

Stir-fried Broccoli

 SERVES 4   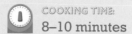 PREP TIME: 5 minutes   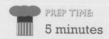 COOKING TIME: 8–10 minutes

nutritional information per serving	121 kcals, 7.5g fat, 1g sat fat, 6g total sugars, 1.3g salt

Broccoli served this way will tempt everyone to try this great dish and is equally delicious made with cauliflower or a combination of the two.

INGREDIENTS

2 tbsp vegetable oil
2 broccoli heads, cut into florets
2 tbsp soy sauce
1 tsp cornflour
1 tbsp caster sugar
1 tsp grated fresh ginger
1 garlic clove, crushed
pinch of dried red pepper flakes
1 tsp toasted sesame seeds, to garnish

1. Heat the oil in a large preheated wok or frying pan over high heat until almost smoking. Add the broccoli and stir-fry for 4–5 minutes. Reduce the heat to medium.

2. Combine the soy sauce, cornflour, sugar, ginger, garlic and red pepper flakes in a small bowl. Add the mixture to the broccoli and cook, stirring constantly, for 2–3 minutes until the sauce thickens slightly.

3. Transfer to a warmed serving dish, garnish with the sesame seeds and serve immediately.

Caramelized Apple & Blue Cheese Salad

 SERVES 2

 PREP TIME:
10 minutes,
plus cooling

 COOKING TIME:
5 minutes

nutritional information per serving	410 kcals, 33g fat, 11g sat fat, 19g total sugars, 0.7g salt

*Apples caramelize better if there are fewer in the pan,
so if you want to make more, cook in batches.*

INGREDIENTS

15 g/½ oz butter

2 tbsp sunflower oil or rapeseed oil

1 large red-skinned dessert apple, such as Pink Lady, cored and cut into thin wedges

2 tsp clear honey

1½ tsp fresh thyme leaves

1½ tbsp white wine vinegar

2 tsp wholegrain mustard

55g/2 oz mixed salad leaves

40 g/1½ oz vegetarian blue cheese, crumbled

25 g/1 oz walnuts, toasted and roughly chopped

2 tbsp snipped chives

salt and pepper

1. Heat the butter with 1 teaspoon of the oil in a frying pan. Add the apples and fry for 2 minutes, stirring occasionally, until soft. Add the honey and thyme and continue to cook until the apples begin to caramelize. Remove from the heat.

2. Stir in the remaining oil, the vinegar and mustard. Season with pepper and a little salt and leave to cool slightly.

3. Place the salad leaves, cheese, walnuts and chives in a serving bowl. Spoon over the apples and warm dressing from the pan. Toss together and serve immediately.

1

2

3

SOMETHING DIFFERENT
You could use firm ripe pears instead of apples, and toasted pine kernels instead of walnuts.

Vegetable & Hazelnut Loaf

 MAKES
1 loaf

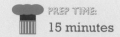 PREP TIME:
15 minutes

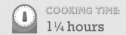 COOKING TIME:
1¼ hours

nutritional information per loaf	1666 kcals, 108g fat, 10g sat fat, 34g total sugars, 5.6g salt

A really popular meatless loaf that's so versatile. Delicious served hot with a tomato sauce or cold with salad.

INGREDIENTS

2 tbsp sunflower oil, plus extra for oiling

1 onion, chopped

1 garlic clove, finely chopped

2 celery sticks, chopped

1 tbsp plain flour

200 ml/7 fl oz strained canned tomatoes

115 g/4 oz fresh wholemeal breadcrumbs

2 carrots, peeled and grated

115 g/4 oz toasted hazelnuts, ground

1 tbsp dark soy sauce

2 tbsp chopped fresh coriander

1 egg, lightly beaten

salt and pepper

mixed red and green lettuce leaves, to serve

1. Preheat the oven to 180°C/350°F/Gas Mark 4. Oil and line a 450-g/1-lb loaf pan. Heat the oil in a heavy-based frying pan. Add the onion and cook over medium heat, stirring frequently, for 5 minutes, or until softened. Add the garlic and celery and cook, stirring frequently, for 5 minutes. Add the flour and cook, stirring, for 1 minute. Gradually stir in the strained canned tomatoes and cook, stirring continuously, until thickened. Remove the pan from the heat.

2. Place the breadcrumbs, carrots, ground hazelnuts, soy sauce and coriander in a bowl. Add the tomato mixture and stir well. Cool slightly, then beat in the egg and season with salt and pepper.

3. Spoon the mixture into the prepared tin and smooth the surface. Cover with foil and bake in the preheated oven for 1 hour. If serving hot, turn the loaf out onto a warmed serving dish and serve with lettuce. Alternatively, cool the loaf in the tin before turning out.

Pepper & Basil Pots

 SERVES 4    PREP TIME: 15 minutes plus chilling   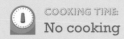 COOKING TIME: No cooking

nutritional information per serving	62 kcals, 1.5g fat, 0.5g sat fat, 10g total sugars, trace salt

A really attractive way to serve layered vegetables. Warm garlic bread goes well for a great starter to a special meal.

INGREDIENTS

1 tsp olive oil

2 shallots, finely chopped

2 garlic cloves, crushed

2 red peppers, peeled, deseeded and sliced into strips

1 orange pepper, peeled, deseeded and sliced into strips

4 tomatoes, thinly sliced

2 tbsp shredded fresh basil, plus extra leaves to garnish

pepper

1. Lightly brush four ramekin dishes with the oil. Mix the shallots and garlic together in a bowl and season with pepper to taste.

2. Layer the red and orange peppers with the tomatoes in the prepared ramekin dishes, sprinkling each layer with the shallot mixture and shredded basil. When all the ingredients have been added, cover lightly with clingfilm or baking paper. Weigh down using small weights and leave in the refrigerator for at least 6 hours, or preferably overnight.

3. When ready to serve, remove the weights and carefully run a knife around the edges. Invert onto serving plates and serve garnished with basil leaves.

SOMETHING DIFFERENT

If you don't have individual dishes, layer the vegetables in a larger dish. To serve, use a sharp knife to slice in wedges.

Potato & Chive Pancakes

 SERVES 4    PREP TIME: 10 minutes   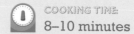 COOKING TIME: 8–10 minutes

nutritional information per serving | 300 kcals, 12g fat, 3g sat fat, 4g total sugars, 1g salt

Delicate pancakes made with grated potato and flavoured with chives make a great light lunch.

INGREDIENTS

150 g/5½ oz plain white flour

1½ tsp baking powder

250 ml/9 fl oz milk

1 large egg

2 tbsp sunflower oil, plus extra for greasing

225 g/8 oz potatoes

2 tbsp snipped chives

1 tbsp wholegrain mustard

salt and pepper

Greek-style yogurt or soured cream, to serve

1. Sift the flour, baking powder and a pinch of salt into a bowl. Add the milk, egg and oil and whisk to a smooth batter.

2. Peel the potatoes and grate coarsely, then place in a colander or sieve and sprinkle with salt. Leave to stand for 5 minutes, then press out as much liquid as possible. Stir the grated potato into the batter with the chives, mustard and pepper to taste.

3. Lightly grease a griddle pan or frying pan and heat over a medium heat. Spoon tablespoons of batter onto the pan and cook until bubbles appear on the surface.

4. Turn over with a palette knife and cook the other side until golden brown. Repeat this process using the remaining batter, while keeping the cooked pancakes warm.

5. Serve immediately, with a spoonful of yogurt.

COOK'S TIP
Best served
freshly made,
keep cooked
pancakes warm
on a baking tray
in a moderate
oven while cooking
the remainder.

Crispy Crêpes with Ratatouille

 SERVES 4   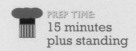 PREP TIME: 15 minutes plus standing   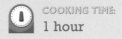 COOKING TIME: 1 hour

nutritional information per serving	410 kcals, 20g fat, 4g sat fat, 9g total sugars, 0.8g salt

A great family dish, just serve with a crisp green salad and crusty bread.

INGREDIENTS

75 g/2¾ oz plain white flour
75 g/2¾ oz plain wholemeal flour
pinch of salt
250 ml/9 fl oz milk
100 ml/3½ fl oz water
1 large egg
2 tbsp olive oil
sunflower oil, for greasing and brushing
4 tbsp dry wholemeal breadcrumbs

filling
3 tbsp olive oil
1 red onion, diced
1 large aubergine, diced
1 garlic clove, crushed
1 large courgette, diced
400 g/14 oz canned chopped tomatoes
2 tbsp chopped fresh oregano
salt and pepper

1. For the filling, heat the oil in a large frying pan over a medium heat, add the onion and aubergine and fry until golden. Add the garlic, courgette, tomatoes and oregano and season to taste with salt and pepper. Cover and simmer for 25–30 minutes, or until tender.

2. Meanwhile, sift the two types of flour and the salt into a bowl, tipping in any bran left in the sieve. Add the milk, water, egg and olive oil and whisk to a smooth, bubbly batter. Leave to stand for 15 minutes.

3. Grease a 20-cm/8-inch frying pan and heat over a medium heat. Pour in enough batter to just cover the pan, swirling to cover in a thin, even layer. Cook until the underside is golden, then flip or turn with a palette knife and cook the other side until golden.

4. Repeat this process using the remaining batter. Interleave the cooked crêpes with kitchen paper and keep warm.

5. Preheat the oven to 200°C/400°F/Gas Mark 6 and grease a wide ovenproof dish.

6. Spoon the filling onto one side of each crêpe and fold over the other side. Arrange in the prepared dish in one layer, brush with oil and sprinkle with breadcrumbs. Bake for 25–30 minutes, until golden. Serve immediately.

1

1

6

Aubergine, Pepper & Basil Crêpe Rolls

 SERVES 4    PREP TIME: 15 minutes plus standing   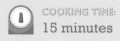 COOKING TIME: 15 minutes

nutritional information per serving	560 kcals, 41g fat, 22g sat fat, 9g total sugars, 0.6g salt

Serve these vegetable and cheese rolls wrapped in paper napkins for fast food at home.

INGREDIENTS

150 g/5½ oz plain white flour
pinch of salt
250 ml/9 fl oz milk
100 ml/3½ fl oz water
1 large egg
2 tbsp olive oil
sunflower oil, for greasing

filling
2 large aubergines
olive oil, for brushing
2 large red peppers, halved and deseeded
250 g/9 oz vegetarian soft cream cheese
handful of fresh basil leaves
salt and pepper

1. For the filling, slice the aubergines lengthwise into 8-mm/⅜-inch thick slices, sprinkle with salt and leave to drain for about 20 minutes. Rinse and dry.

2. Preheat the grill to high. Arrange the aubergine slices on a baking sheet in a single layer, brush with olive oil and grill until golden, turning once. Arrange the red peppers, cut side down, on a baking sheet in a single layer and grill until blackened. Remove the skins and slice.

3. Sift the flour and salt into a bowl. Add the milk, water, egg and oil and whisk to a smooth, bubbly batter. Leave to stand for 15 minutes.

4. Lightly grease a 20-cm/8-inch frying pan and heat over a medium heat. Pour in enough batter to just cover the pan, swirling to cover in a thin, even layer. Cook until the underside is golden, then flip or turn with a palette knife and cook the other side until golden brown.

5. Repeat this process using the remaining batter. Interleave the cooked crêpes with kitchen paper and keep warm.

6. Arrange the pancakes in pairs, slightly overlapping. Spread with cheese and top with the aubergines, red peppers, basil and salt and pepper to taste. Roll up firmly from one short side. Cut in half diagonally and serve immediately.

Feta & Spinach Tartlets

 MAKES 6

 PREP TIME:
15 minutes
plus chilling

 COOKING TIME:
25 minutes

nutritional information per tartlet	478 kcals, 41g fat, 22g sat fat, 2g total sugars, 1.2g salt

These tartlets are perfect for a picnic alongside celery, carrot sticks and a spicy salsa for dipping.

INGREDIENTS

pastry
125 g/4½ oz plain flour, plus extra for dusting
pinch of salt
75 g/2¾ oz cold butter, cut into pieces, plus extra for greasing
½ tsp ground nutmeg
1–2 tbsp cold water

filling
250 g/9 oz baby spinach
25 g/1 oz butter
150 ml/5 fl oz double cream
3 egg yolks
125 g/4½ oz vegetarian feta cheese
50 g/1¾ oz pine kernels
salt and pepper

1. Grease six 9-cm/3½-inch loose-based round tart tins. Sift the flour and salt into a food processor, add the butter and process until the mixture resembles fine breadcrumbs. Tip the mixture into a large bowl and add the nutmeg and enough cold water to bring the dough together.

2. Turn out the dough onto a floured surface and divide into six equal-sized pieces. Roll each piece to fit the tart tins. Carefully fit each piece of pastry in its case and press well to fit the tin. Roll the rolling pin over the tin to neaten the edges and trim the excess pastry. Cut out six pieces of baking paper and fit a piece into each tart, fill with baking beans and chill in the refrigerator for 30 minutes.

3. Preheat the oven to 200°C/400°F/Gas Mark 6. Bake the tart cases blind in the preheated oven for 10 minutes, then remove the beans and paper.

4. Blanch the spinach in boiling water for just 1 minute, then drain and press to squeeze all the water out. Chop the spinach. Melt the butter in a frying pan, add the spinach and cook gently to evaporate any remaining liquid. Season well with salt and pepper. Stir in the cream and egg yolks. Crumble the cheese and divide between the tarts, top with the spinach mixture and bake for 10 minutes. Scatter the pine kernels over the tartlets and cook for a further 5 minutes.

5. Let rest in the tart tins for 5 minutes, then gently turn the tartlets out onto a wire rack to cool. Serve warm or cold.

Lattice Flan

 SERVES 8

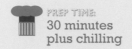 PREP TIME:
30 minutes
plus chilling

 COOKING TIME:
60 minutes

nutritional information per serving	483 kcals, 32g fat, 17g sat fat, 3g total sugars, 1.1g salt

The perfect combination of spinach and ricotta encased in crispy shortcrust pastry.

INGREDIENTS

rich shortcrust pastry
350 g/12 oz plain flour, plus extra for dusting

pinch of salt

175 g/6 oz butter, diced, plus extra for greasing

2 egg yolks

6 tbsp ice-cold water

filling
450 g/1 lb frozen spinach, thawed

2 tbsp olive oil

1 large onion, chopped

2 garlic cloves, finely chopped

2 eggs, lightly beaten

225 g/8 oz vegetarian ricotta cheese

55 g/2 oz freshly grated vegetarian Parmesan-style cheese

pinch of freshly grated nutmeg

salt and pepper

1. To make the pastry, sift the flour with the salt into a bowl. Add the butter and rub into the flour with your fingertips until the mixture resembles fine breadcrumbs. Beat the egg yolks with the water in a small bowl. Sprinkle the liquid over the flour mixture and combine with a round-bladed knife to form a dough. Shape into a ball, wrap in foil and chill in the refrigerator for 30 minutes.

2. To make the filling, drain the spinach and squeeze out as much moisture as possible. Heat the oil in a large, heavy-based frying pan over a medium heat. Add the onion and cook, stirring frequently, for 5 minutes, or until softened. Add the garlic and spinach and cook, stirring occasionally, for 10 minutes. Remove from the heat and leave to cool slightly, then beat in the eggs (reserving a little for glazing), the ricotta and the grated cheese. Season to taste with salt and pepper and nutmeg.

3. Preheat the oven to 200°C/400°F/Gas Mark 6. Lightly grease a 23-cm/9-inch loose-based flan tin. Roll out two-thirds of the dough on a lightly floured work surface and use to line the tin. Spoon in the spinach mixture, spreading it evenly over the base.

4. Roll out the remaining dough on a lightly floured work surface and cut into 5-mm/¼-inch strips. Arrange the strips in a lattice pattern on top of the flan, pressing the ends securely to seal. Trim any excess pastry. Brush with the egg to glaze and bake in the preheated oven for 45 minutes, or until golden brown. Transfer to a wire rack to cool slightly before removing from the tin.

Glazed Beetroot & Egg Sourdough Toasties

 SERVES 4   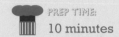 PREP TIME: 10 minutes    COOKING TIME: 12–15 minutes

nutritional information **per serving**   404 kcals, 24g fat, 4g sat fat, 14g total sugars, 1.4g salt

Try this traditional combination of ruby red beetroot and chopped egg served on sourdough bread for a great lunch dish.

INGREDIENTS

4 eggs

500 g/1 lb 2 oz cooked beetroot (fresh or vacuum-packed without vinegar)

2 tsp sugar

5 tsp cider vinegar

4 slices sourdough bread (from a long oval loaf)

6 tbsp olive oil

1 tbsp Dijon mustard

3 tbsp chopped fresh dill, plus extra sprigs to garnish

salt and pepper

1. Boil the eggs for 8 minutes, then drain, shell and chop them. Set aside. Dice the beetroot quite small and place in a small bowl. Mix in half the sugar, 1 tsp of the cider vinegar and seasoning.

2. Preheat the grill to a medium–high setting. Brush the bread with a little olive oil and toast on one side on the rack in the grill pan for 2–3 minutes, until crisp and golden.

3. Meanwhile, trickle 1 tsp of the remaining oil over the beetroot. Whisk the remaining cider vinegar, mustard and remaining sugar together with seasoning. Gradually whisk in the remaining oil to make a thick dressing. Stir in the dill and taste for seasoning – it should be sweet and mustardy, with a sharpness – add more sugar or vinegar if you wish.

4. Turn the bread and top with the beetroot, giving it a stir first, covering the slices right up to the crusts. Glaze the beetroot under the grill for 2–3 minutes, until browned in places.

5. Cut the slices in half or quarters and top with egg. Drizzle with a little dressing, garnish with the dill sprigs and serve immediately.

Tomato Tarte Tatin

 SERVES 4    PREP TIME: 15 minutes    COOKING TIME: 25–30 minutes

nutritional information per serving	557 kcals, 35g fat, 22g sat fat, 9g total sugars, 0.7g salt

An inspirational savoury twist on the French classic dessert made with apples.

INGREDIENTS

25 g/1 oz butter
1 tbsp caster sugar
500 g/1 lb 2 oz cherry tomatoes, halved
1 garlic clove, crushed
2 tsp white wine vinegar
salt and pepper

pastry
250 g/9 oz plain flour, sifted
pinch of salt
140 g/5 oz butter
1 tbsp chopped oregano, plus extra to garnish
5–6 tbsp cold water

1. Preheat the oven to 200°C/400°F/Gas Mark 6. Melt the butter in a heavy-based frying pan. Add the sugar and stir over a fairly high heat until just turning golden brown.

2. Remove from the heat and quickly add the tomatoes, garlic and white wine vinegar, stirring to coat evenly. Season with salt and pepper. Tip the tomatoes into a 23-cm/9-inch cake tin, spreading evenly.

3. For the pastry, place the flour, salt, butter and oregano in a food processor and process until the mixture resembles fine breadcrumbs. Add just enough water to bind to a soft, but not sticky, dough.

4. Roll out the pastry to a 25-cm/10-inch round and place over the tomatoes, tucking in the edges. Pierce with a fork to let out steam.

5. Bake in the preheated oven for 25–30 minutes, until firm and golden. Rest for 2–3 minutes, then run a knife around the edge and turn out onto a warm serving plate. Sprinkle the tarte tatin with chopped oregano and serve warm.

Risotto with Asparagus & Walnuts

 SERVES 4    PREP TIME: 5 minutes    COOKING TIME: 20–25 minutes

nutritional information per serving	550 kcals, 20g fat, 4g sat fat, 2.5g total sugars, trace salt

Welcome Spring with this classic rice dish and use the freshest asparagus you can find.

INGREDIENTS

15 g/½ oz butter
3 tbsp olive oil
1 small onion, finely chopped
350 g/12 oz risotto rice
150 ml/5 fl oz dry white wine
1.5 litres/2¾ pints hot vegetable stock
200 g/7 oz asparagus tips, cut into 6-cm/2½-inch lengths
40 g/1½ oz chopped walnuts
grated rind of 1 lemon
salt and pepper
walnut oil, to serve (optional)
strips of lemon zest, to garnish

1. Heat the butter and olive oil in a large saucepan and fry the onion, stirring, for 3–4 minutes, until softened. Add the rice and stir over a medium heat for 1 minute, without browning. Add the wine and boil rapidly, stirring, until almost all the wine has evaporated.

2. Stir the stock into the pan a ladleful at a time, allowing each ladleful to be absorbed before adding more. After 10 minutes, add the asparagus and continue cooking, adding stock when necessary. After a further 5 minutes, test a grain of rice – it should be 'al dente' or firm to the bite.

3. Stir in the walnuts and lemon rind, then adjust the seasoning, adding salt and pepper to taste. Remove from the heat and drizzle over a little walnut oil, if using, stirring in lightly. Serve the risotto immediately, garnished with strips of lemon zest.

Spicy Polenta with Poached Eggs

 SERVES 4   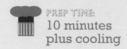 PREP TIME: 10 minutes plus cooling   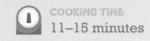 COOKING TIME: 11–15 minutes

nutritional information per serving	414 kcals, 24g fat, 11g sat fat, 1g total sugars, 1g salt

To use the polenta trimmings, chop roughly, place in a shallow ovenproof dish, brush with melted butter and grill for 3 minutes. Serve as an unusual side dish.

INGREDIENTS

oil, for oiling
600 ml/1 pint water
150 g/5½ oz polenta
85 g/3 oz freshly grated vegetarian Parmesan-style cheese
40 g/1½ oz butter
½–1 red chilli, deseeded and very finely chopped
200 g/7 oz baby spinach leaves, or a mixture of baby spinach leaves and rocket leaves
2 tsp white wine vinegar
4 large eggs
salt and pepper

1. Lightly oil an 18-cm/7-inch square cake tin. Bring the water to the boil in a saucepan. Add the polenta in a thin stream and cook, stirring, over a medium–low heat for 3 minutes until thick. Stir in 55 g/2 oz of the cheese, 30 g/1 oz of the butter and the chilli. Working quickly, transfer to the prepared tin and level the surface. Set aside for 30 minutes until cool and firm, then cut out four rounds with a 9-cm/3½-inch cutter and transfer to a baking tray.

2. Wash the spinach and place in a large saucepan with the water clinging to the leaves. Cover and cook for 2–3 minutes until wilted, then squeeze out the excess water between two plates. Return to the pan.

3. Preheat the grill to high. Sprinkle the polenta rounds with the remaining cheese, place under the preheated grill and cook for 3 minutes until brown and bubbling on the top. Keep warm. Meanwhile, add the remaining butter and salt and pepper to taste to the spinach and heat through.

4. Half fill a saucepan with water, add the vinegar and bring to simmering point. Crack the eggs into cups and slide gently into the water. Cook over a low heat, without allowing the water to boil, for 3 minutes until the whites are firm and the yolk is still soft. Scoop out with a slotted spoon and drain briefly on kitchen paper.

5. To serve, place the polenta rounds on four warmed plates and divide the spinach between them. Top with the eggs and sprinkle with a little salt and pepper. Serve immediately.

1

1

3

Chilli Broccoli Pasta *168*

Griddled Courgette & Feta Pizza *170*

Spicy Aubergine, Chickpea & Coriander Penne *172*

Lentil Bolognese *174*

Rigatoni with Roast Courgette, Tomato & Mascarpone Sauce *176*

Sichuan Mixed Vegetables *178*

Satay Noodles *180*

Teriyaki Tofu Stir-Fry *182*

New Potato, Feta & Herb Frittata *184*

Caponata *186*

Bean & Vegetable Chilli *188*

Pasta with Two Cheeses & Walnuts *190*

Mediterranean Vegetables with Feta & Olives *192*

Kashmiri Vegetables *194*

Red Curry with Mixed Leaves *196*

Quinoa with Roasted Vegetables *198*

Stir-Fried Rice with Green Vegetables *200*

Bean Burgers *202*

Leek, Herb & Mushroom Risotto *204*

Ricotta, Spinach & Pine Kernel Pizza *206*

Smoky Mushroom & Coriander Burgers *208*

Mixed Nut Roast with Cranberry & Red Wine Sauce *210*

Mushroom & Onion Quiche *212*

Chinese Greens Curry *214*

Main Meals

Chilli Broccoli Pasta

 SERVES 4   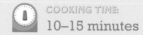 PREP TIME: 5 minutes    COOKING TIME: 10–15 minutes

nutritional information per serving	300 kcals, 11g fat, 1.5g sat fat, 3g total sugars, trace salt

A dish made with these ingredients can't fail – they just seem right together. Good for serving to a crowd.

INGREDIENTS

225 g/8 oz dried penne or macaroni

225 g/8 oz head of broccoli, cut into florets

50 ml/2 fl oz extra virgin olive oil

2 large garlic cloves, chopped

2 fresh red chillies, deseeded and diced

8 cherry tomatoes

handful of fresh basil leaves, to garnish

salt

1. Bring a large saucepan of lightly salted water to the boil. Add the pasta, return to the boil and cook for 8–10 minutes, until tender but still firm to the bite. Drain the pasta, refresh under cold running water and drain again. Set aside.

2. Bring a separate saucepan of lightly salted water to the boil, add the broccoli and cook for 5 minutes. Drain, refresh under cold running water and drain again.

3. Heat the oil in a large, heavy-based frying pan over high heat. Add the garlic, chillies and tomatoes and cook, stirring constantly, for 1 minute.

4. Add the broccoli and mix well. Cook for 2 minutes, stirring, to heat through. Add the pasta and mix well again. Cook for a further minute. Transfer the pasta to a large, warmed serving bowl and serve immediately, garnished with basil leaves.

Griddled Courgette & Feta Pizza

 MAKES
2 pizzas

 PREP TIME:
20 minutes
plus rising

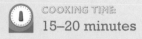 COOKING TIME:
15–20 minutes

nutritional information per pizza	996 kcals, 42g fat, 20g sat fat, 10g total sugars, 8.6g salt

However easy it is to send out for pizza, you can't beat the taste and texture of the dough when you make it yourself.

INGREDIENTS

basic pizza dough
300 g/10½ oz strong white flour, plus extra for dusting
1 tsp easy-blend dried yeast
1½ tsp salt
175 ml/6 fl oz hand-hot water
1 tbsp olive oil, plus extra for kneading

topping
1 tbsp olive oil
1 garlic clove, crushed
1 large courgette, sliced lengthways
200 g/7 oz ready-prepared tomato pizza sauce
250 g/9 oz vegetarian feta cheese, drained and crumbled
salt and pepper
fresh mint leaves, roughly torn, to garnish

1. Sift the flour into a mixing bowl and add the yeast and salt, making a small well in the top. Mix the water and oil together and pour into the bowl, using a round-bladed knife to gradually combine all the flour to make a sticky dough.

2. Lightly flour the work surface and your hands and knead the dough for about 10 minutes, until it is smooth and elastic.

3. Cover the dough with some lightly oiled clingfilm or a damp tea towel and leave to rise for about an hour, or until it has doubled in size.

4. Knock back the dough by gently kneading for about a minute, then divide into two balls. To roll out the dough, flatten each ball, then, using a rolling pin, roll out on a lightly floured work surface, giving a quarter turn between each roll.

5. Preheat the oven to 220°C/425°F/Gas Mark 7. Place the pizza bases on two baking trays, using a rolling pin to transfer them from the work surface.

6. Heat the oil in a griddle pan over a medium heat. Add the garlic and courgette and cook over a medium heat for 4–5 minutes, turning regularly, until softened and chargrilled. Remove with a slotted spoon and drain on kitchen paper.

7. Divide the pizza sauce between the two pizza bases, spreading almost to the edges. Place the courgette slices on the pizza bases, scatter with the cheese and season to taste with salt and pepper. Bake in the preheated oven for 10–12 minutes, or until the cheese is turning golden and the bases are crisp underneath. Garnish with the fresh mint and serve immediately.

6

7

7

Spicy Aubergine, Chickpea & Coriander Penne

 SERVES 4    PREP TIME: 10 minutes    COOKING TIME: 30 minutes

nutritional information per serving	428 kcals, 9.5g fat, 1.3g sat fat, 11g total sugars, 0.5g salt

Made mainly from storecupboard ingredients, this can be whipped-up in a flash and your guests will love it.

INGREDIENTS

large pinch of saffron threads

450 ml/16 fl oz hot vegetable stock

2 tbsp olive oil

1 large onion, roughly chopped

1 tsp cumin seeds, crushed

350 g/12 oz aubergine, diced

1 large red pepper, deseeded and chopped

400 g/14 oz canned chopped tomatoes with garlic

1 tsp ground cinnamon

30 g/1 oz fresh coriander, leaves and stalks separated and roughly chopped

400 g/14 oz canned chickpeas, drained and rinsed

280 g/10 oz dried penne

salt and pepper

harissa or chilli sauce, to serve

1. Toast the saffron threads in a dry frying pan set over a medium heat for 20–30 seconds, just until they begin to give off their aroma. Place in a small bowl and crumble with your fingers. Add 2 tablespoons of the hot stock and set aside to infuse.

2. Heat the oil in a large saucepan. Add the onion and fry for 5–6 minutes, until golden brown. Add the cumin and fry for a further 20–30 seconds, then stir in the aubergine, red pepper, tomatoes, cinnamon, coriander stalks, saffron liquid and remaining stock. Cover and simmer for 20 minutes.

3. Add the chickpeas to the saucepan and season to taste with salt and pepper. Simmer for a further 5 minutes, removing the lid to reduce and thicken the sauce if necessary.

4. Meanwhile, bring a large, heavy-based saucepan of lightly salted water to the boil. Add the pasta, return to the boil and cook for 8–10 minutes, or until tender but still firm to the bite. Drain and transfer to a warmed serving bowl. Add the sauce and half the coriander leaves, then toss. Garnish with the remaining coriander and serve immediately with the harissa or chilli sauce.

Lentil Bolognese

 SERVES 4　　 PREP TIME: 15 minutes　　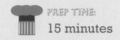 COOKING TIME: 45–55 minutes

nutritional information per serving	500 kcals, 8g fat, 1g sat fat, 16.5g total sugars, 0.3g salt

No vegetarian kitchen should be without a recipe for this popular pasta sauce.

INGREDIENTS

175 g/6 oz green lentils

2 tbsp olive oil

1 large onion, chopped

2 garlic cloves, crushed

2 carrots, chopped

2 celery sticks, chopped

800 g/1 lb 12 oz canned chopped tomatoes

150 ml/5 fl oz vegetable stock

1 red pepper, deseeded and chopped

2 tbsp tomato purée

2 tsp very finely chopped fresh rosemary

1 tsp dried oregano

280 g/10 oz dried spaghetti or linguine

handful of basil leaves, torn

salt and pepper

freshly grated vegetarian Parmesan-style cheese, to serve

1. Put the lentils in a saucepan and cover with cold water. Bring to the boil and simmer for 20–30 minutes until just tender. Drain well.

2. Meanwhile, heat the oil in a large saucepan. Add the onion, garlic, carrots and celery. Cover and cook over a low heat for 5 minutes. Stir in the tomatoes, stock, red pepper, tomato purée, rosemary and oregano. Cover and simmer for 20 minutes until the sauce is thickened and the vegetables are tender. Add the lentils and cook, stirring, for a further 5 minutes. Season with salt and pepper.

3. While the sauce is cooking, bring a large saucepan of lightly salted water to the boil. Add the spaghetti, bring back to the boil and cook for 10 minutes, or until tender but still firm to the bite. Drain well, then divide the spaghetti between four warmed bowls. Spoon the sauce over the top and scatter with the basil leaves. Serve immediately with the grated cheese on the side.

Sichuan Mixed Vegetables

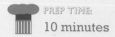 SERVES 4

 PREP TIME:
10 minutes

COOKING TIME:
10 minutes

nutritional information per serving	200 kcals, 18g fat, 2g sat fat, 11g total sugars, 2.2g salt

Smooth or crunchy peanut butter can be used for this recipe which will give the vegetables their authentic taste.

INGREDIENTS

2 tbsp chilli oil

4 garlic cloves, crushed

5-cm/2-inch piece grated fresh ginger

250 g/9 oz carrots, cut into thin strips

1 red pepper, cut into thin strips

150 g/5½ oz shiitake mushrooms, sliced

150 g/5½ oz mangetout, halved diagonally

3 tbsp soy sauce

3 tbsp peanut butter

350 g/12 oz beansprouts

cooked rice, to serve

1. Heat the chilli oil in a preheated wok and fry the garlic, ginger and carrots for 3 minutes. Add the red pepper and stir-fry for another 2 minutes.

2. Add the mushrooms and mangetout and stir-fry for 1 minute.

3. In a small bowl, mix together the soy sauce and peanut butter until combined.

4. Using a wooden spoon, make a space in the centre of the stir-fried vegetables so that the base of the wok is visible. Pour in the sauce and bring to the boil, stirring all the time until it starts to thicken. Add the beansprouts and toss the vegetables to coat thoroughly with the sauce.

5. Transfer to a warmed serving dish and serve immediately with freshly cooked rice.

SOMETHING
DIFFERENT
This dish will
taste equally good
if served with
either egg or rice
noodles.

Satay Noodles

 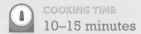
nutritional information
per serving   775 kcals, 52g fat, 27g sat fat, 10g total sugars, 3.3g salt

An easy, filling meal for days when you're almost too busy to cook – and there's only one pot to wash up.

INGREDIENTS

125 g/4½ oz dried medium egg noodles

85 g/3 oz creamed coconut, chopped

150 ml/5 fl oz boiling water

2 tsp oil

1 large red pepper, deseeded and thinly sliced

1 plump garlic clove, thinly sliced

125 g/4½ oz beansprouts

2 tbsp dark soy sauce

55 g/2 oz roasted salted peanuts, roughly chopped

3 spring onions, diagonally sliced

large handful of coriander leaves, chopped

salt

2 lime halves, to serve

1. Bring a large saucepan of lightly salted water to the boil. Add the noodles, bring back to the boil and cook for 4 minutes, or until tender but still firm to the bite. Drain. Add the creamed coconut to the boiling water and stir until dissolved.

2. Heat the oil in a wok or a large, heavy-based frying pan. Add the pepper and stir-fry over a high heat for 2–3 minutes until soft. Add the garlic and stir-fry for a further 40–60 seconds, taking care that it doesn't burn.

3. Add the beansprouts, followed by the noodles, dissolved coconut, soy sauce and peanuts. Reduce the heat and stir for a further 2–3 minutes until piping hot. Add the spring onions and coriander and toss together.

4. Divide between two warmed bowls and serve immediately with the lime halves for squeezing over.

Teriyaki Tofu Stir-fry

 SERVES 2　　 PREP TIME: 15 minutes　　 COOKING TIME: 15 minutes

nutritional information **per serving** — 738 kcals, 25g fat, 4g sat fat, 33g total sugars, 4.6g salt

Try this method of dry-frying tofu which firms up the texture without adding extra calories and fat.

INGREDIENTS

140 g/5 oz medium egg noodles

200 g/7 oz firm tofu, drained

2 tbsp sunflower oil or vegetable oil

1 red pepper, deseeded and thinly sliced

140 g/5 oz baby corn, diagonally sliced

200 g/7 oz choi sum, cut into 4-cm/1½-inch pieces

salt

sauce

3 tbsp tamari or dark soy sauce

3 tbsp rice wine

3 tbsp clear honey

1 tbsp cornflour

1 tbsp finely grated fresh ginger

1–2 garlic cloves, crushed

250 ml/9 fl oz water

1. Bring a large saucepan of lightly salted water to the boil. Add the noodles, bring back to the boil and cook for 4 minutes, or until tender but still firm to the bite. Drain.

2. Meanwhile, cut the tofu into 15-mm/⅝-inch slices and then into bite-sized pieces. Pat dry on plenty of kitchen paper. Heat a non-stick or well-seasoned frying pan over a medium–low heat, then add the tofu and cook for 3 minutes, without moving the pieces around the pan, until golden brown underneath. Turn and cook for a further 2–3 minutes on the other side. Transfer to a plate.

3. To make the sauce, mix the tamari, rice wine, honey, cornflour, ginger and garlic together in a jug until well blended, then stir in the water. Set aside.

4. Heat the oil in a wok or a large, heavy-based frying pan. Add the pepper and baby corn, and stir-fry for 3 minutes. Add the choi sum and stir-fry for a further 2 minutes. Pour in the sauce and heat, stirring constantly, until it boils and thickens. Add the noodles and tofu and toss together over the heat for a further 1–2 minutes until heated through. Serve immediately.

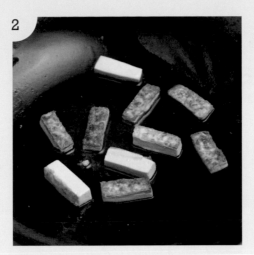

Caponata

 SERVES 4    PREP TIME: 10 minutes plus cooling   COOKING TIME: 20 minutes

nutritional information per serving	190 kcals, 13g fat, 2g sat fat, 12g total sugars, 1.2g salt

A great dish from Sicily, where the exact combination of ingredients is endlessly debated. This recipe is one of the most popular.

INGREDIENTS

4 tbsp olive oil

2 celery sticks, sliced

2 red onions, sliced

450 g/1 lb aubergines, diced

1 garlic clove, finely chopped

5 plum tomatoes, chopped

3 tbsp red wine vinegar

1 tbsp sugar

3 tbsp stoned green olives

2 tbsp capers

4 tbsp chopped fresh flat-leaf parsley

salt and pepper

ciabatta bread, to serve

1. Heat half the oil in a large, heavy-based saucepan. Add the celery and onions and cook over a low heat, stirring occasionally, for 5 minutes, until softened but not coloured. Add the remaining oil and the aubergines. Cook, stirring frequently, for about 5 minutes, until the aubergine starts to colour.

2. Add the garlic, tomatoes, vinegar and sugar and mix well. Cover the mixture with a circle of greaseproof paper and simmer gently for about 10 minutes.

3. Remove the greaseproof paper, stir in the olives and capers and season to taste with salt and pepper. Pour into a serving dish and set aside to cool to room temperature. When cool, sprinkle over the parsley and serve immediately with ciabatta bread.

GOES WELL WITH
When not served as a dish in its own right, Caponata can be incorporated into a multitude of recipes. Add to pasta, use to top bruschetta or mix into scrambled eggs.

Pasta with Two Cheeses & Walnuts

 SERVES 4    PREP TIME: 5 minutes    COOKING TIME: 15 minutes

nutritional information per serving	838 kcals, 49g fat, 20g sat fat, 5g total sugars, 0.9g salt

The perfect dish to eat curled up on the sofa watching TV. Alternatively, it makes a brilliant supper dish in a more formal setting served with a crisp salad and a glass of wine.

INGREDIENTS

350 g/12 oz dried penne

280 g/10 oz fresh or frozen peas

150 g/5½ oz vegetarian soft cheese with garlic and herbs

175 g/6 oz baby spinach leaves

100 g/3½ oz vegetarian blue cheese, cut into small cubes

115 g/4 oz walnuts, roughly chopped

salt and pepper

1. Cook the pasta in a large saucepan of lightly salted boiling water for 8–10 minutes, adding the peas for the final 2 minutes. Drain, reserving 125 ml/4 fl oz of the hot cooking liquid.

2. Return the pan to the heat. Add the reserved cooking liquid and the soft cheese. Heat, stirring, until melted and smooth.

3. Remove from the heat, then add the spinach to the pan followed by the pasta, peas, blue cheese and walnuts. Season to taste with pepper and toss together, until the spinach has wilted and the cheese has started to melt. Serve immediately.

1

2

3

Mediterranean Vegetables with Feta & Olives

 SERVES 4

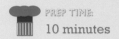 PREP TIME:
10 minutes

 COOKING TIME:
20–25 minutes

nutritional information per serving	240 kcals, 12g fat, 2.5g sat fat, 11g total sugars, 0.7g salt

Let the wonderful aromas wafting from the kitchen remind you of warm evenings dining alfresco.

INGREDIENTS

1 red onion, sliced into thick rings

1 small aubergine, thickly sliced

2 large mushrooms, halved

3 red peppers, halved and deseeded

3 plum tomatoes, peeled and diced

2 garlic cloves, very finely chopped

1 tbsp chopped fresh flat-leaf parsley

1 tsp chopped fresh rosemary

1 tsp dried thyme or oregano

finely grated rind of 1 lemon

75 g/2¾ oz stale, coarse breadcrumbs

3 tbsp olive oil, plus extra for brushing

6–8 black olives, stoned and sliced

25 g/1 oz vegetarian feta cheese (drained weight), cut into 1-cm/½-inch cubes

salt and pepper

1. Preheat the grill to medium. Put the onion, aubergine, mushrooms and peppers on a large baking tray, placing the peppers cut-side down. Brush with a little oil. Cook under the preheated grill for 10–12 minutes, turning the onion, aubergine and mushrooms halfway through, until beginning to blacken. Cut into even-sized chunks.

2. Preheat the oven to 220°C/425°F/Gas Mark 7. Place the grilled vegetables in a shallow ovenproof dish and arrange the tomatoes on top. Season to taste with salt and pepper.

3. In a bowl, combine the garlic, parsley, rosemary, thyme and lemon rind with the breadcrumbs. Season to taste with pepper. Add the oil to bind the mixture together. Scatter the breadcrumb mixture over the vegetables, followed by the olives and feta cheese.

4. Bake in the preheated oven for 10–15 minutes, or until the vegetables are heated through and the topping is crisp. Serve immediately.

1

2

3

Kashmiri Vegetables

 SERVES 4  PREP TIME: 10 minutes  COOKING TIME: 30 minutes

nutritional information
per serving   303 kcals, 15g fat, 2.5g sat fat, 7g total sugars, 0.12g salt

If you've never tried okra before this is a great recipe to start with. As it cooks, a sticky juice is released but this will gradually be absorbed as you stir the mixture.

INGREDIENTS

3 tbsp ghee or vegetable oil
2 tbsp flaked almonds
8 cardamom seeds
8 black peppercorns
2 tsp cumin seeds
1 cinnamon stick
2 fresh green chillies, deseeded and chopped
1 tsp ginger paste
1 tsp chilli powder
3 potatoes, cut into chunks
225 g/8 oz okra, cut into 2.5-cm/1-inch pieces
½ cauliflower, broken into florets
150 ml/5 fl oz natural yogurt
150 ml/5 fl oz vegetable stock or water
salt
freshly cooked rice, to serve

1. Heat 1 tablespoon of the ghee in a heavy-based saucepan. Add the almonds and cook over a low heat, stirring constantly, for 2 minutes, or until golden.

2. Remove the almonds from the saucepan with a slotted spoon, drain on kitchen paper and set aside. Place the cardamom seeds, peppercorns, cumin seeds and cinnamon stick in a spice grinder or mortar and grind finely.

3. Add the remaining ghee to the saucepan and heat. Add the green chillies and cook, stirring frequently, for 2 minutes. Stir in the ginger paste, chilli powder and ground spices and cook, stirring constantly, for 2 minutes, or until they give off their aroma.

4. Add the potatoes, season with salt to taste. Cover and cook, stirring occasionally, for 8 minutes. Add the okra and cauliflower and cook for a further 5 minutes.

5. Gradually stir in the yogurt and stock and bring to the boil. Cover and simmer for a further 10 minutes, until all the vegetables are tender. Garnish with the reserved flaked almonds and serve with freshly cooked rice.

1

2

5

Red Curry with Mixed Leaves

 SERVES 4    PREP TIME: 10 minutes    COOKING TIME: 10 minutes

nutritional information per serving	304 kcals, 25g fat, 16g sat fat, 6g total sugars, 0.5g salt

Have your rice cooked ready for serving as this fantastic, coconut milk flavoured, vegetable curry is quickly cooked in a wok.

INGREDIENTS

2 tbsp groundnut oil or vegetable oil

2 onions, thinly sliced

1 bunch of fine asparagus spears

400 ml/14 fl oz coconut milk

2 tbsp red curry paste

3 fresh kaffir lime leaves

225 g/8 oz baby spinach leaves

2 heads pak choi, chopped

1 small head Chinese leaves, shredded

handful of fresh coriander, chopped

freshly cooked rice, to serve

1. Heat a wok over a medium–high heat and add the oil. Add the onions and asparagus and stir-fry for 1–2 minutes.

2. Add the coconut milk, curry paste and lime leaves and bring gently to the boil, stirring occasionally.

3. Add the spinach, pak choi and Chinese leaves and cook, stirring, for 2–3 minutes, until wilted. Add the coriander and stir well. Serve immediately with freshly cooked rice.

Quinoa with Roasted Vegetables

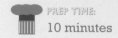 SERVES 2

 PREP TIME: 10 minutes

 COOKING TIME: 40–45 minutes

nutritional information per serving	418 kcals, 23g fat, 2g sat fat, 14g total sugars, 0.1g salt

Quinoa (pronounced keen-wah) is an ancient grain originating from South America.

INGREDIENTS

2 peppers (any colour), deseeded and cut into chunky pieces

1 large courgette, cut into chunks

1 small fennel bulb, cut into slim wedges

1 tbsp olive oil

2 tsp very finely chopped fresh rosemary

1 tsp chopped fresh thyme

100 g/3½ oz quinoa

350 ml/12 fl oz vegetable stock

2 garlic cloves, crushed

3 tbsp chopped fresh flat leaf parsley

40 g/1½ oz pine kernels, toasted

salt and pepper

1. Preheat the oven to 200°C/400°F/Gas Mark 6. Place the peppers, courgette and fennel in a roasting tin large enough to hold the vegetables in a single layer.

2. Drizzle the olive oil over the vegetables and scatter with the rosemary and thyme. Season well with salt and pepper and mix well with clean hands. Roast for 25–30 minutes until tender and lightly charred.

3. Meanwhile, place the quinoa, stock and garlic in a saucepan. Bring to the boil, cover and simmer for 12–15 minutes until tender and most of the stock has been absorbed.

4. Remove the vegetables from the oven. Tip the quinoa into the roasting tin. Add the parsley and pine kernels and toss together. Serve warm or cold.

SOMETHING DIFFERENT
If you're unable to buy highly nutritious quinoa (although it's a very popular grain these days) use brown basmati rice instead.

Stir-Fried Rice with Green Vegetables

 SERVES 4

 PREP TIME:
5 minutes
plus cooling

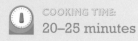 COOKING TIME:
20–25 minutes

nutritional information
per serving · 288 kcals, 7g fat, 0.8g sat fat, 3g total sugars, 0.2g salt

Thai basil should not be confused with sweet basil used in many Italian dishes. Thai basil has a slight liquorice flavour which complements this dish perfectly.

INGREDIENTS

225 g/8 oz jasmine rice
2 tbsp vegetable or peanut oil
1 tbsp green curry paste
6 spring onions, sliced
2 garlic cloves, crushed
1 courgette, cut into thin sticks
115 g/4 oz French beans
175 g/6 oz asparagus, trimmed
3–4 fresh Thai basil leaves

1. Cook the rice in lightly salted boiling water for 12–15 minutes, drain well, cover, cool thoroughly and chill.

2. Heat the oil in a wok and stir-fry the curry paste for 1 minute. Add the spring onions and garlic and stir-fry for 1 minute.

3. Add the courgette, beans and asparagus and stir-fry for 3–4 minutes, until just tender. Break up the rice and add it to the wok. Cook, stirring constantly for 2–3 minutes, until the rice is hot. Stir in the basil and serve immediately.

FREEZING TIP
Thai basil can be frozen in small quantities. Chop the leaves in a food processor adding a little vegetable oil to coat. Pack into ice cube trays and freeze.

Bean Burgers

 PREP TIME:
15 minutes

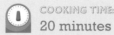 COOKING TIME:
20 minutes

nutritional information per serving	111 kcals, 4g fat, 0.5g sat fat, 3.5g total sugars, 0.6g salt

Satisfy your appetite with these great tasting home-made burgers that will taste far better than those you buy.

INGREDIENTS

1 tbsp sunflower oil, plus extra for brushing

1 onion, finely chopped

1 garlic clove, finely chopped

1 tsp ground coriander

1 tsp ground cumin

115 g/4 oz white mushrooms, finely chopped

425 g/15 oz canned borlotti or red kidney beans, drained and rinsed

2 tbsp chopped fresh flat-leaf parsley

plain flour, for dusting

salt and pepper

hamburger buns and salad, to serve

1. Heat the oil in a heavy-based frying pan over a medium heat. Add the onion and cook, stirring frequently, for 5 minutes, or until softened. Add the garlic, coriander and cumin and cook, stirring, for a further minute. Add the mushrooms and cook, stirring frequently, for 4–5 minutes until all the liquid has evaporated. Transfer to a bowl.

2. Put the beans in a small bowl and mash with a fork. Stir into the mushroom mixture with the parsley and season with salt and pepper.

3. Preheat the grill to medium–high. Divide the mixture equally into four portions, dust lightly with flour and shape into flat, round burgers. Brush with oil and cook under the grill for 4–5 minutes on each side. Serve in hamburger buns with salad.

BE PREPARED
These will freeze
well so make
a double batch.
Open freeze
on a tray then
transfer to a
rigid container.
Freeze for up to
3 months. Cook
from frozen.

Leek, Herb & Mushroom Risotto

 SERVES 8  PREP TIME: 15 minutes  COOKING TIME: 30–35 minutes

nutritional information per serving	243 kcals, 8.5g fat, 4g sat fat, 0.5g total sugars, 0.2g salt

A filling and comforting dish. Use a mixture of cultivated and wild mushrooms rather than chestnut mushrooms, if you prefer.

INGREDIENTS

1 litre/1¾ pints hot vegetable stock

2 tbsp olive oil

1 small leek, roughly chopped

3 garlic cloves, crushed

1 tbsp fresh thyme

250 g/9 oz chestnut mushrooms, sliced

300 g/10½ oz arborio rice

175 ml/6 fl oz dry white wine

30 g/1 oz butter

55 g/2 oz freshly grated vegetarian Parmesan-style cheese

2 tbsp snipped fresh chives, plus extra to serve

salt and pepper

rocket leaves and vegetarian Parmesan-style cheese shavings, to garnish

1. Keep the stock hot in a saucepan set over a medium heat. Heat the oil in a separate saucepan over a low heat. Add the leek, garlic and thyme and cook for 5 minutes until soft. Add the mushrooms and continue to cook for a further 4 minutes until soft.

2. Stir in the rice and cook stirring for 1 minute, then add the wine and heat rapidly until the liquid has almost completely evaporated.

3. Add a ladleful of stock and cook over a medium heat, stirring, until it is absorbed by the rice. Continue adding the stock in the same way until it is all used up and the rice is creamy, plump and tender.

4. If the risotto is a little undercooked add a splash of water and continue cooking until creamy. Adding extra stock may make the risotto too salty.

5. Stir in the butter, followed by the cheese and chives. Season with salt and pepper. Serve in warmed bowls topped with rocket leaves, chives and cheese shavings.

Ricotta, Spinach & Pine Kernel Pizza

 MAKES
1 pizza

 PREP TIME:
20 minutes
plus rising

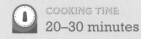 COOKING TIME:
20–30 minutes

nutritional information per pizza	2601kcals, 187g fat, 82g sat fat, 16g total sugars, 9.5g salt

Ricotta and fontina are two famous Italian cheeses and are the perfect combination for this great-tasting pizza.

INGREDIENTS

basic pizza dough
200 g/7 oz strong white flour, plus extra for dusting
1 tsp easy-blend dried yeast
1 tsp salt
6 tbsp hand-hot water
1 tbsp olive oil, plus extra for kneading

topping
350 g/12 oz spinach
2 tbsp olive oil, plus extra for brushing and drizzling
1 onion, thinly sliced
6 tbsp vegetarian ricotta cheese
½ tsp freshly grated nutmeg
2 tbsp pine kernels
115 g/4 oz vegetarian fontina cheese, sliced thinly
salt and pepper

1. Sift the flour into a mixing bowl and add the yeast and salt, making a small well in the top. Mix the water and oil together and pour into the bowl, using a round-bladed knife to gradually combine all the flour to make a sticky dough.

2. Lightly flour the work surface and your hands and knead the dough for about 10 minutes, until it is smooth and elastic.

3. Cover the dough with some lightly oiled clingfilm or a damp tea towel and leave to rise for about an hour, or until it has doubled in size.

4. Preheat the oven to 220°C/425°F/Gas Mark 7. Brush a baking sheet with oil.

5. Roll out the dough on a lightly floured surface to a 25-cm/10-inch round. Place on the baking sheet and push up the edge a little. Cover and let stand in a warm place for 10 minutes.

6. Wash the spinach in cold water and dry well. Heat the oil in a pan, add the onion and cook until soft and translucent. Add the spinach and cook, stirring, until just wilted. Remove the pan from the heat and drain off any liquid.

7. Spread the ricotta cheese evenly over the pizza base, then cover with the spinach and onion mixture. Sprinkle over the nutmeg and pine kernels and season to taste with salt and pepper. Top with the slices of fontina and drizzle with olive oil. Bake in the preheated oven for 20–30 minutes, until golden and sizzling. Serve immediately.

5

6

7

Smoky Mushroom & Coriander Burgers

 SERVES 6

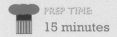 PREP TIME: 15 minutes

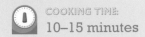 COOKING TIME: 10–15 minutes

nutritional information per serving	170 kcals, 6g fat, 0.8g sat fat, 5g total sugars, 1.8g salt

Children will love helping mix and shape these vegan burgers.

INGREDIENTS

425 g/15 oz canned red kidney beans, rinsed and drained

2 tbsp sunflower oil or vegetable oil, plus extra for brushing

1 onion, finely chopped

115 g/4 oz mushrooms, finely chopped

1 large carrot, coarsely grated

2 tsp smoked paprika

70 g/2½ oz porridge oats

3 tbsp dark soy sauce

2 tbsp tomato purée

30 g/1 oz fresh coriander, including stalks, chopped

3 tbsp plain flour

salt and pepper

to serve
soft rolls

salad leaves

sliced avocado

tomato salsa or relish

1. Place the beans in a large bowl and mash as thoroughly as you can with a potato masher. Heat the oil in a frying pan, add the onion and fry for 2 minutes until translucent. Add the mushrooms, carrot and paprika and fry for a further 4 minutes until the vegetables are soft.

2. Add the fried vegetables to the beans with the oats, soy sauce, tomato purée and coriander. Season with salt and pepper and mix well. Divide into six equal portions and shape into burgers, then turn in the flour to coat lightly.

3. Preheat a griddle pan until smoking. Lightly brush the tops of the burgers with oil, then place oiled side down on the pan. Cook over a medium heat for 2–3 minutes until lightly charred underneath. Lightly brush the tops with oil, turn and cook for a further 2-3 minutes on the other side. Serve hot in soft rolls with salad leaves, avocado slices and salsa.

1

2

3

Mixed Nut Roast with Cranberry & Red Wine Sauce

 MAKES
1 loaf

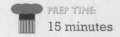 PREP TIME:
15 minutes

 COOKING TIME:
30 minutes

nutritional information per loaf	711 kcals, 45g fat, 8.5g sat fat, 31g total sugars, 0.7g salt

Serve with roast carrots, parsnips and potatoes for an alternative Christmas feast.

INGREDIENTS

2 tbsp butter, plus extra for greasing

2 garlic cloves, chopped

1 large onion, chopped

50 g/1¾ oz pine kernels, toasted

75 g/2¾ oz hazelnuts, toasted

50 g/1¾ oz walnuts, ground

50 g/1¾ oz cashew nuts, ground

100 g/3½ oz fresh wholemeal breadcrumbs

1 egg, lightly beaten

2 tbsp chopped fresh thyme, plus extra sprigs to garnish

250 ml/9 fl oz vegetable stock

salt and pepper

cranberry & red wine sauce

175 g/6 oz fresh cranberries

100 g/3½ oz caster sugar

300 ml/10 fl oz red wine

1 cinnamon stick

1. Preheat the oven to 180°C/350°F/Gas Mark 4. Grease a loaf tin and line it with greaseproof paper. Melt the butter in a saucepan over a medium heat. Add the garlic and onion and cook, stirring, for about 3 minutes. Remove the pan from the heat. Grind the pine kernels and hazelnuts. Stir all the nuts into the pan and add the breadcrumbs, egg, thyme, stock and salt and pepper to taste.

2. Spoon the mixture into the loaf tin and level the surface. Cook in the centre of the preheated oven for 30 minutes or until cooked through and golden. The loaf is cooked when a skewer inserted into the centre comes out clean.

3. Halfway through the cooking time, make the cranberry and red wine sauce. Put all the ingredients in a saucepan and bring to the boil. Reduce the heat and simmer, stirring occasionally, for 15 minutes.

4. Remove the nut roast from the oven and turn out. Garnish with sprigs of thyme and serve with the cranberry and red wine sauce.

Mushroom & Onion Quiche

 SERVES 4   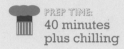 PREP TIME:
40 minutes
plus chilling   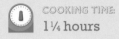 COOKING TIME:
1¼ hours

nutritional information per serving	650 kcals, 50g fat, 29g sat fat, 5g total sugars, 0.7g salt

Baking the empty pastry case first ensures a crisp base to this flavour packed savoury tart.

INGREDIENTS

rich shortcrust pastry
175 g/6 oz plain flour, plus extra for dusting
pinch of salt
85 g/3 oz butter, diced, plus extra for greasing
1 egg yolk
3 tbsp ice-cold water

filling
55 g/2 oz unsalted butter
3 red onions, halved and sliced
350 g/12 oz mixed wild mushrooms, such as ceps, chanterelles and morels
2 tsp chopped fresh thyme
1 egg
2 egg yolks
100 ml/3½ fl oz double cream
salt and pepper

1. Sift the flour with the salt into a bowl. Add the butter and rub into the flour with your fingertips until the mixture resembles fine breadcrumbs. Beat the egg yolk with the water in a small bowl. Sprinkle the liquid over the flour mixture and combine with a round-bladed knife to form a dough. Shape into a ball, wrap in foil and chill in the refrigerator for 30 minutes.

2. Preheat the oven to 190°C/375°F/Gas Mark 5. Lightly grease a 23-cm/9-inch loose-based quiche tin. Roll out the dough on a lightly floured work surface and use to line the tin. Line the pastry case with baking paper and fill with baking beans. Bake in the preheated oven for 25 minutes. Remove the paper and beans and cool on a wire rack. Reduce the oven temperature to 180°C/350°F/Gas Mark 4.

3. To make the filling, melt the butter in a large, heavy-based frying pan over a very low heat. Add the onions, cover and cook, stirring occasionally, for 20 minutes. Add the mushrooms and thyme and cook, stirring occasionally, for a further 10 minutes. Spoon into the pastry case and put the tin on a baking tray.

4. Lightly beat the egg, egg yolks, cream and salt and pepper to taste in a bowl. Pour over the mushroom mixture. Bake in the oven for 20 minutes, or until the filling is set and golden. Serve hot or at room temperature.

2

3

3

Chinese Greens Curry

 SERVES 4

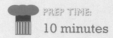 PREP TIME:
10 minutes

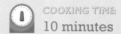 COOKING TIME:
10 minutes

nutritional information
per serving | 507 kcals, 28g fat, 17.3g sat fat, 44.8g total sugars, 0.4g salt

*The combination of Chinese and Thai flavourings results
in a light and fresh tasting vegetable dish.*

INGREDIENTS

2 tbsp vegetable or groundnut oil

1 fresh green chilli, deseeded and chopped

6 spring onions, sliced

3 tbsp green curry paste

115 g/4 oz pak choi

115 g/4 oz Chinese leaves

115 g/4 oz spinach

115 g/4 oz asparagus

3 celery sticks, sliced diagonally

3 tbsp Thai soy sauce

1 tsp palm sugar or soft light brown sugar

juice of 1 lime

freshly cooked jasmine rice, to serve

1. Heat the oil in a wok or large frying pan and stir-fry the chilli and spring onions for 1–2 minutes. Add the curry paste and stir-fry for 2–3 minutes.

2. Add the pak choi, Chinese leaves, spinach, asparagus and celery and stir-fry for 3–4 minutes, until just tender.

3. Add the soy sauce, sugar and lime juice and cook for 30 seconds to heat through. Serve immediately with freshly cooked jasmine rice.

1

2

3

SOMETHING
DIFFERENT
Ring the
changes with the
vegetables you
choose for this
recipe and try
adding coconut
milk to create
more sauce.

Baked Lemon Cheesecake *218*

Pecan Pie *220*

Amaretti & Peaches *222*

Sweet Pumpkin Pie *224*

Key Lime Pie *226*

Stuffed Baked Apples *228*

Grilled Pineapple with Nutty Yogurt *230*

Peach & Amaretto Crêpes *232*

Grilled Fruit Kebabs *234*

Baked Apricots with Honey *236*

Prosecco Sorbet with Grapes *238*

Butterscotch, Mango & Ginger Sundaes *240*

White Wine & Honey Syllabub *242*

Chocolate Orange Tart *244*

Raspberry Croissant Puddings *246*

Baked Passion Fruit Custards *248*

Almond Meringues with Summer Berries *250*

Baked Spicy Pudding *252*

Apple Fritters *254*

Sweet Peach Delight *256*

Strawberry & Cream Whoopie Pies *258*

Apple Pie Pizza *260*

Apple & Lime Sorbet *262*

Rhubarb Shortcake Crumble *264*

Desserts

Baked Lemon Cheesecake

 SERVES 8    PREP TIME:
15 minutes
plus chilling    COOKING TIME:
40–45 minutes

nutritional information per serving	316 kcals, 17g fat, 10g sat fat, 22g total sugars, 0.5g salt

Try this lighter version of everyone's favourite cheesecake and then you won't feel so guilty having a second piece!

INGREDIENTS

55 g/2 oz butter,
plus extra for greasing

175 g/6 oz gingernut
biscuits, crushed

3 lemons

300 g/10½ oz vegetarian ricotta
cheese

200 g/7 oz Greek-style yogurt

4 eggs

1 tbsp cornflour

100 g/3½ oz caster sugar

strips of lemon zest and icing
sugar, to decorate

1. Preheat the oven to 180°C/350°F/Gas Mark 4. Grease a 20-cm/8-inch round springform cake tin and line with baking paper.

2. Melt the butter and stir in the biscuit crumbs. Press into the base of the prepared cake tin. Chill until firm.

3. Meanwhile, finely grate the rind and squeeze the juice from the lemons. Add the ricotta, yogurt, eggs, cornflour and caster sugar, and whisk until a smooth batter is formed.

4. Carefully spoon the mixture into the tin. Bake in the preheated oven for 40–45 minutes, or until just firm and golden brown.

5. Cool the cheesecake completely in the tin, then run a knife around the edge to loosen and turn out onto a serving plate. Decorate with lemon zest and dust with icing sugar.

2

3

5

GOES WELL WITH
A selection of
fresh ripe berries
that have had a
dash of cassis
stirred into them.

Pecan Pie

 SERVES 8

 PREP TIME:
15 minutes
plus chilling

 COOKING TIME:
50–55 minutes

nutritional information per serving	500 kcals, 32g fat, 14g sat fat, 30g total sugars, 0.2g salt

This traditional American pie is believed to have been created by the first French settlers in New Orleans.

INGREDIENTS

pastry
200 g/7 oz plain flour, plus extra for dusting
115 g/4 oz unsalted butter
2 tbsp caster sugar
a little cold water

filling
70 g/2½ oz unsalted butter
100 g/3½ oz light muscovado sugar
140 g/5 oz golden syrup
2 large eggs, beaten
1 tsp vanilla extract
115 g/4 oz pecan nuts

1. For the pastry, place the flour in a bowl and rub in the butter with your fingertips until it resembles fine breadcrumbs. Stir in the caster sugar and add enough cold water to mix to a firm dough. Wrap in clingfilm and chill for 15 minutes, until firm enough to roll out.

2. Preheat the oven to 200°C/400°F/Gas Mark 6. Roll out the pastry on a lightly floured surface and use to line a 23-cm/9-inch loose-based round tart tin. Prick the base with a fork. Chill for 15 minutes.

3. Place the tart tin on a baking sheet and line with baking paper and baking beans. Bake blind in the preheated oven for 10 minutes. Remove the baking beans and paper and bake for a further 5 minutes. Reduce the oven temperature to 180°C/350°F/Gas Mark 4.

4. For the filling, place the butter, muscovado sugar and golden syrup in a saucepan and heat gently until melted. Remove from the heat and quickly beat in the eggs and vanilla extract. Roughly chop the pecan nuts and stir into the mixture. Pour into the pastry case and bake for 35–40 minutes, until the filling is just set.

3

4

4

Amaretti & Peaches

 SERVES 6   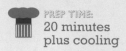 PREP TIME: 20 minutes plus cooling   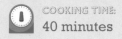 COOKING TIME: 40 minutes

nutritional information per serving	263 kcals, 13g fat, 4g sat fat, 29g total sugars, 0.1g salt

Delicious crisp, almond-tasting biscuits go perfectly with peaches and ice cream and are also great with an espresso coffee.

INGREDIENTS

1 egg white
85 g/3 oz caster sugar
85 g/3 oz ground almonds
a few drops of almond extract
3 peaches or nectarines, sliced
2 tbsp almond liqueur
300 g/10½ oz vanilla ice cream (6 scoops)

1. Preheat the oven to 160°C/325°F/Gas Mark 3. Line a baking sheet with baking paper.

2. Place the egg white in a large bowl and whisk until stiff. Gently fold the sugar, ground almonds and almond extract into the egg white with a large metal spoon until you have a smooth paste.

3. Roll teaspoonfuls of the mixture lightly between the palms of your hands to form 12 walnut-sized balls. Place the balls 2 cm/¾ inch apart on the prepared baking sheet. Bake in the preheated oven for approximately 20 minutes until cracked and light golden. Remove the biscotti from the oven, and leave to cool, but keep the oven on.

4. Meanwhile, place the sliced peaches and 1 tablespoon of the almond liqueur in a heatproof dish. Cover and bake in the preheated oven for 20 minutes until just tender. Remove from the oven, sprinkle with the remaining almond liqueur and leave to cool.

5. Drain the peaches, reserving the juices, and arrange the peach slices in a fan on six side plates. Sandwich a scoop of ice cream between two amaretti and place on top of each peach fan. Spoon over the reserved peach juices and serve immediately.

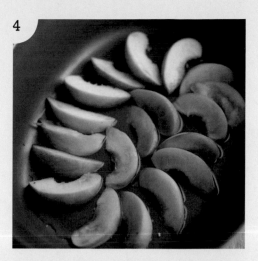

Sweet Pumpkin Pie

 SERVES 8    PREP TIME:
30 minutes
plus chilling   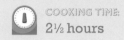 COOKING TIME:
2½ hours

nutritional information per serving	575 kcals, 31g fat, 11g sat fat, 46g total sugars, 0.9g salt

With a nutty streusel topping, this is the pumpkin pie to beat them all. Serve with cream for a dessert to remember.

INGREDIENTS

1.8 kg/4 lb sweet pumpkin, halved and deseeded, stem and stringy bits removed

140 g/5 oz plain flour, plus extra for dusting

¼ tsp baking powder

1½ tsp ground cinnamon

¾ tsp ground nutmeg

¾ tsp ground cloves

1 tsp salt

50 g/1¾ oz caster sugar

55 g/2 oz cold unsalted butter, diced, plus extra for greasing

3 eggs

400 ml/14 fl oz canned condensed milk

½ tsp vanilla extract

1 tbsp demerara sugar

streusel topping
2 tbsp plain flour

4 tbsp demerara sugar

1 tsp ground cinnamon

2 tbsp cold unsalted butter, diced

75 g/2¾ oz pecan nuts, chopped

75 g/2¾ oz walnuts, chopped

1. Preheat the oven to 190°C/375°F/Gas Mark 5. Put the pumpkin halves, face down, in a shallow baking tin and cover with foil. Bake in the preheated oven for 1½ hours, then leave to cool. Scoop out the flesh and purée in a food processor. Drain off any excess liquid. Cover and chill.

2. Grease a 23-cm/9-inch round tart tin. To make the pastry, sift the flour and baking powder into a large bowl. Stir in ½ teaspoon of the cinnamon, ¼ teaspoon of the nutmeg, ¼ teaspoon of the cloves, ½ teaspoon of the salt and all the caster sugar. Rub in the butter with your fingertips until the mixture resembles fine breadcrumbs, then make a well in the centre. Lightly beat one of the eggs and pour it into the well. Mix together with a wooden spoon, then shape the dough into a ball. Place the dough on a lightly floured surface, roll out and use to line the prepared tin. Trim the edges, then cover and chill for 30 minutes.

3. Preheat the oven to 220°C/425°F/Gas Mark 7. Put the pumpkin purée in a large bowl, then stir in the condensed milk and the remaining eggs. Add the remaining spices and salt, then stir in the vanilla extract and demerara sugar. Pour into the pastry case and bake in the preheated oven for 15 minutes.

4. Meanwhile, make the topping. Mix the flour, demerara sugar and cinnamon in a bowl, rub in the butter, then stir in the nuts. Remove the pie from the oven and reduce the heat to 180°C/350°F/Gas Mark 4. Sprinkle over the topping, then bake for a further 35 minutes. Remove from the oven and serve hot or cold.

2

3

4

Key Lime Pie

 SERVES 8

 PREP TIME:
20 minutes
plus chilling

 COOKING TIME:
20 minutes

nutritional information per serving	385 kcals, 20g fat, 11g sat fat, 33g total sugars, 0.7g salt

This pie is from Florida, famous for its delicious tart limes.

INGREDIENTS

biscuit crust
175 g/6 oz digestive or ginger biscuits

2 tbsp caster sugar

½ tsp ground cinnamon

70 g/2½ oz butter, melted, plus extra for greasing

filling
400 g/14 oz canned condensed milk

125 ml/4 fl oz freshly squeezed lime juice

finely grated rind of 3 limes

4 egg yolks

whipped cream, to serve

1. Preheat the oven to 160°C/325°F/Gas Mark 3. Grease a 23-cm/9-inch round tart tin, about 4 cm/1½ inches deep.

2. To make the biscuit crust, put the biscuits, sugar and cinnamon in a food processor and process until fine crumbs form – do not overprocess to a powder. Add the melted butter and process again until moistened.

3. Tip the crumb mixture into the prepared tart tin and press evenly into the base and sides. Place the tart tin on a baking sheet and bake in the preheated oven for 5 minutes. Meanwhile, beat the condensed milk, lime juice, lime rind and egg yolks together in a bowl until well blended.

4. Remove the tart tin from the oven, pour the filling into the biscuit crust and spread out to the edges. Return to the oven for a further 15 minutes, or until the filling is set around the edges but still wobbly in the centre. Leave to cool completely on a wire rack, then cover and chill for at least 2 hours. Serve spread thickly with whipped cream.

3

3

4

SOMETHING DIFFERENT
If you don't have time to make the biscuit crust, bake the filling in a ready-made short crust case.

Stuffed Baked Apples

 SERVES 4   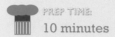 PREP TIME: 10 minutes   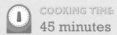 COOKING TIME: 45 minutes

nutritional information per serving	241 kcals, 5g fat, 0.5g sat fat, 35g total sugars, trace salt

There's nothing more comforting than a baked apple and stuffed with plump apricots, ginger and honey, this recipe is the best.

INGREDIENTS

25 g/1 oz blanched almonds

55 g/2 oz ready-to-eat plumped dried apricots

1 piece stem ginger, drained

1 tbsp clear honey

1 tbsp syrup from the stem ginger jar

4 tbsp rolled oats

4 large Bramley apples

1. Preheat the oven to 180°C/350°F/Gas Mark 4. Using a sharp knife, chop the almonds, apricots and stem ginger very finely. Set aside until needed.

2. Place the honey and syrup in a saucepan and heat until the honey has melted. Stir in the oats and cook gently over low heat for 2 minutes. Remove the saucepan from the heat and stir in the almonds, apricots and stem ginger.

3. Core the apples, widen the tops slightly and score horizontally around the circumference of each to prevent the skins bursting during cooking. Place the apples in an ovenproof dish and fill the cavities with the stuffing. Pour just enough water into the dish to come about one-third of the way up the apples. Bake in the preheated oven for 40 minutes, or until tender. Serve immediately.

1

2

3

SOMETHING
DIFFERENT
For a change use
dried cranberries
or mixed fruit
and pecans or
walnuts.

Grilled Pineapple with Nutty Yogurt

 SERVES 4

 PREP TIME:
15 minutes

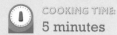 COOKING TIME:
5 minutes

nutritional information per serving	296 kcals, 20.2g fat, 1.5g sat fat, 21g total sugars, trace salt

Not just for serving cold in a fruit salad, pineapple makes a quick and easy, warm dessert when grilled. Also try sprinkling the slices with cinnamon and brown sugar, wrapping in foil and cooking on the barbecue.

INGREDIENTS

1 fresh pineapple

sunflower oil, for brushing

150 ml/5 fl oz reduced-fat Greek-style yogurt

115 g/4 oz hazelnuts, skinned and roughly chopped

1. Cut off the leaf top from the pineapple and discard. Cut the pineapple into slices 2 cm/¾ inches thick. Using a sharp knife, cut off the skin from each slice, then, holding the slices on their sides, cut out and discard the 'eyes'. Stamp out the core with an apple corer or biscuit cutter and cut each slice in half.

2. Brush the grill rack with oil and preheat the grill to high. Mix the yogurt and hazelnuts together in a bowl and set aside until needed.

3. Arrange the pineapple slices on the grill rack and cook under the preheated grill for 3–5 minutes until golden. Serve with the nutty yogurt.

1

1

2

BE PREPARED
Cutting the pineapple can be quite tricky so give yourself plenty of time and make sure you have a sharp knife.

Peach & Amaretto Crêpes

 SERVES 4

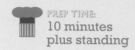 PREP TIME: 10 minutes plus standing

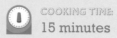 COOKING TIME: 15 minutes

nutritional information per serving	524 kcals, 23g fat, 11g sat fat, 37g total sugars, 0.7g salt

Amaretto is a centuries-old Italian liqueur flavoured with almonds. It goes particularly well with peaches.

INGREDIENTS

150 g/5½ oz plain white flour
pinch of salt
250 ml/9 fl oz milk
100 ml/3½ fl oz peach nectar or orange juice
1 large egg
2 tbsp melted butter
butter, for greasing
55 g/2 oz amaretti, crumbled, to serve

filling
40 g/1½ oz butter
2 ripe peaches, sliced
55 g/2 oz caster sugar
4 tbsp amaretto

1. Sift the flour and salt into a bowl. Add the milk, peach nectar, egg and butter and whisk to a smooth, bubbly batter. Leave to stand for 15 minutes.

2. Lightly grease a 20-cm/8-inch frying pan and heat over a medium heat. Pour in enough batter to just cover the pan, swirling to cover in a fairly thin, even layer. Cook until the underside is golden, then flip or turn with a palette knife and cook the other side until golden brown.

3. Repeat this process using the remaining batter. Interleave the cooked crêpes with kitchen paper and keep warm. For the filling, melt the butter in a wide saucepan over a fairly high heat and add the peaches. Sprinkle with sugar and cook for 2–3 minutes, stirring, until golden. Add the amaretto and remove from the heat.

4. Divide the peaches between the crêpes and fold over. Spoon over the peach juices, sprinkle with crushed amaretti and serve immediately.

1

1

3

SOMETHING
DIFFERENT
You could
serve bananas in
the same way
using brown
sugar and dark
rum instead.

Grilled Fruit Kebabs

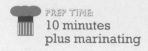 SERVES 4

PREP TIME:
10 minutes
plus marinating

COOKING TIME:
10 minutes

nutritional information per serving	164 kcals, 8g fat, 0.5g sat fat, 22g total sugars, trace salt

Apart from small berries, most fruits can be grilled this way. Choose firm fruit so they stay in place.

INGREDIENTS

2 tbsp hazelnut oil

2 tbsp clear honey

juice and finely grated rind of 1 lime

2 pineapple rings, cut into chunks

8 strawberries

1 pear, peeled, cored and thickly sliced

1 banana, peeled and thickly sliced

2 kiwi fruit, peeled and quartered

1. Preheat the grill to medium. Mix the oil, honey and lime juice and rind together in a large, shallow, non-metallic dish. Add the fruit and turn to coat. Cover and leave to marinate for 10 minutes.

2. Thread the fruit alternately onto four long metal skewers, beginning with a piece of pineapple and ending with a strawberry.

3. Brush the kebabs with the marinade and cook under the grill, brushing frequently with the marinade, for 5 minutes. Turn the kebabs over, brush with the remaining marinade and grill for a further 5 minutes. Serve at once.

1
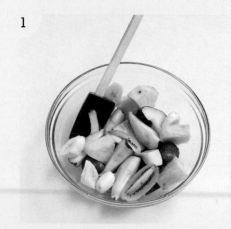

2
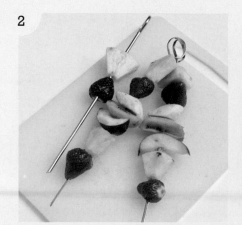

3

Baked Apricots with Honey

 SERVES 4   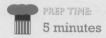 PREP TIME: 5 minutes   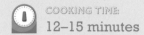 COOKING TIME: 12–15 minutes

nutritional information per serving	161 kcals, 1.5g fat, 0.7g sat fat, 35g total sugars, trace salt

The season for fresh golden apricots is short so take full advantage when you see them in the market. This simple recipe really brings out their flavour.

INGREDIENTS

butter, for greasing
4 apricots, halved and stoned
4 tbsp flaked almonds
4 tbsp honey
pinch of ground ginger or grated nutmeg
vanilla ice cream, to serve (optional)

1. Preheat the oven to 200°C/400°F/Gas Mark 6. Lightly grease an ovenproof dish large enough to hold the apricot halves in a single layer.

2. Arrange the apricot halves in the dish, cut-sides up. Sprinkle with the almonds and drizzle over the honey. Dust with the ginger.

3. Bake in the preheated oven for 12–15 minutes until the apricots are tender and the almonds golden. Remove from the oven and serve at once, with ice cream on the side, if desired.

1

2

3

Prosecco Sorbet
with Grapes

 SERVES 4　　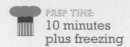 PREP TIME:
10 minutes
plus freezing　　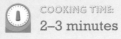 COOKING TIME:
2–3 minutes

nutritional information per serving	213 kcals, 0g fat, 0g sat fat, 42g total sugars, trace salt

A deliciously light and summery sorbet that's really easy to make.

INGREDIENTS

150 g/5½ oz caster sugar
150 ml/5 fl oz water
thinly pared strip of lemon zest
juice of 1 lemon
350 ml/12 fl oz prosecco
grapes and fresh mint sprigs, to decorate

1. Place the sugar and water in a pan with the lemon zest. Stir over a low heat until the sugar dissolves, then boil for 2–3 minutes to reduce by half. Leave to cool and remove the lemon zest.

2. Combine the syrup with the lemon juice and prosecco, then churn the mixture in an ice-cream maker following the manufacturer's instructions. Alternatively, pour into a freezerproof container and freeze, uncovered, whisking at hourly intervals until frozen.

3. When ready to serve, leave at room temperature to soften slightly, then scoop the sorbet into sundae glasses.

1

2

3

TO SERVE
Decorate with grapes
and mint sprigs
before serving.

Butterscotch, Mango & Ginger Sundaes

 SERVES 4 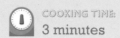 PREP TIME: 10 minutes 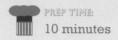 COOKING TIME: 3 minutes

nutritional information per serving	1122 kcals, 70g fat, 40g sat fat, 98g total sugars, 0.8g salt

A pretty dessert for a celebration. If you don't have sundae dishes why not serve this recipe in wine glasses?

INGREDIENTS

1 large, ripe mango
115 g/4 oz ginger biscuits
1 litre/1¾ pints vanilla ice cream
2 tbsp roughly chopped almonds, toasted

sauce

100 g/3½ oz light muscovado sugar
100 g/3½ oz golden syrup
55 g/2 oz unsalted butter
100 ml/3½ fl oz double cream
½ tsp vanilla extract

1. To make the butterscotch sauce, melt the sugar, golden syrup and butter in a small pan and simmer for 3 minutes, stirring, until smooth. Stir in the cream and vanilla extract, then remove from the heat.

2. Peel and stone the mango and cut into 1-cm/½-inch cubes.

3. Place the ginger biscuits in a polythene bag and crush lightly with a rolling pin.

4. Place half the mango in four sundae dishes and top each with a scoop of the ice cream. Spoon over a little butterscotch sauce and sprinkle with crushed biscuits. Repeat with the remaining ingredients.

5. Sprinkle some of the almonds over the top of each sundae and serve immediately.

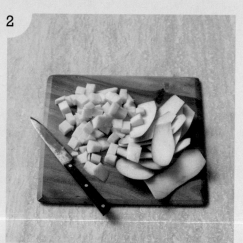

White Wine & Honey Syllabub

 SERVES 4   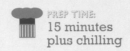 PREP TIME: 15 minutes plus chilling   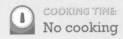 COOKING TIME: No cooking

nutritional information per serving | 947 kcals, 88g fat, 51g sat fat, 25g total sugars, trace salt

This traditional English dessert made from whipped cream can be flavoured in many ways. Serve in small portions with delicate sponge fingers or brandy snaps.

INGREDIENTS

3 tbsp brandy
3 tbsp white wine
600 ml/1 pint double cream
6 tbsp clear honey
55 g/2 oz flaked almonds

1. Combine the brandy and wine in a bowl.

2. Pour the cream into a separate large bowl and whip until just thickened. Add the honey to the cream and whip for about 15 seconds.

3. Pour the brandy and wine mixture in a continuous stream into the cream and honey mixture, whipping constantly, until the mixture forms soft peaks.

4. Spoon into serving dishes. Transfer to the refrigerator and leave to chill for 2–3 hours. Scatter over the flaked almonds and serve.

2

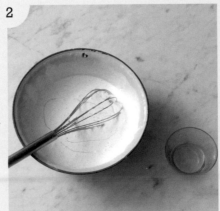

2

3

SOMETHING
DIFFERENT
Instead of brandy
you could use sweet
sherry or Madeira
wine and add a little
grated lemon zest too.

Chocolate Orange Tart

 SERVES 6

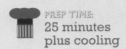 PREP TIME:
25 minutes
plus cooling

 COOKING TIME:
35–45 minutes

nutritional information per serving	421 kcals, 24g fat, 11g sat fat, 27g total sugars, 0.6g salt

This dessert is a safe bet for a celebration (who doesn't love chocolate, after all?) and you can get ahead by making it the day before.

INGREDIENTS

200 g/7 oz ready-made sweet pastry

100 g/3½ plain chocolate, at least 70 per cent cocoa solids, broken into pieces

55 g/2 oz butter, cut into pieces

85 g/3 oz soft light brown sugar

2 large eggs

finely grated zest of 1 large orange

30 g/1 oz plain flour, plus extra for dusting

3 tbsp orange juice

2 clementines, peeled and thinly sliced (optional), and cocoa powder, to decorate

crème fraîche, to serve

1. Thinly roll out the pastry on a lightly floured surface and use to line a 22-cm/8½-inch tart tin. Chill for 20 minutes.

2. Meanwhile, preheat the oven to 200°C/400°F/Gas Mark 6. Line the pastry case with baking paper and fill with ceramic baking beans. Bake in the preheated oven for 15 minutes, then remove the beans and paper and return to the oven for a further 5–10 minutes to crisp the base.

3. Put the chocolate and butter in a heatproof bowl set over a saucepan of gently simmering water and heat, stirring occasionally, until melted and smooth. Place the sugar, eggs and orange zest in a separate bowl and whisk together until frothy and the sugar has dissolved completely. Sift the flour over the top. Add the melted chocolate mixture and the orange juice and stir together until completely smooth.

4. Pour into the pastry case and return to the oven for 15–20 minutes until the filling is just set in the middle. Cool for at least 30 minutes, then remove from the tin. Serve warm or chill overnight – the filling will become dense and truffle-like. To serve, sift a little cocoa powder over the top of the tart and decorate with sliced clementines, if using. Serve with crème fraîche.

Raspberry Croissant Puddings

 SERVES 4

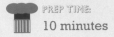 PREP TIME: 10 minutes

 COOKING TIME: 20 minutes

nutritional information per serving	441 kcals, 25.5g fat, 13g sat fat, 18g total sugars, 0.9g salt

An up-market version of bread and butter pudding and a great way to use up stale croissants – should you ever have any!

INGREDIENTS

30 g/1 oz unsalted butter, melted

4 croissants

225 g/8 oz fresh raspberries

4 tbsp maple syrup

350 ml/12 fl oz milk

2 large eggs, beaten

1 tsp vanilla extract

freshly grated nutmeg, for sprinkling

1. Preheat the oven to 220°C/425°F/Gas Mark 7. Place a baking tray on the middle shelf. Brush four 350-ml/12-fl oz ovenproof dishes with half the butter.

2. Chop the croissants into bite-sized chunks. Mix with the raspberries and divide between the dishes. Spoon 1 tablespoon of the maple syrup over the contents of each dish.

3. Heat the milk until almost boiling, then quickly beat in the eggs and vanilla extract. Pour the milk mixture evenly over the dishes, pressing the croissants down lightly. Drizzle with the remaining butter and sprinkle a little nutmeg over each dish.

4. Place the dishes on the baking tray and bake in the preheated oven for about 20 minutes, until lightly set. Serve hot.

Almond Meringues with Summer Berries

 SERVES 6

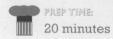 PREP TIME:
20 minutes

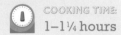 COOKING TIME:
1–1¼ hours

nutritional information per serving	529 kcals, 44g fat, 25g sat fat, 28g total sugars, 0.1g salt

This pretty meringue and cream dessert makes a change from pavlova and it's much easier to serve.

INGREDIENTS

2 large egg whites

115 g/4 oz soft light brown sugar

40 g/1½ oz flaked almonds

450 ml/16 fl oz double cream

2–3 tbsp rosewater, depending on strength, or 3 tbsp dry white wine

1 tbsp icing sugar

500 g/1 lb 2 oz prepared mixed summer fruit, such as hulled and halved strawberries, stoned cherries, blueberries, raspberries, redcurrants, blackberries and blackcurrants

1. Preheat the oven to 120°C/250°F/Gas Mark ½. Line two baking trays with non-stick baking paper. Place the egg whites in a large, grease-free bowl. Whisk with an electric mixer until stiff, then whisk in the brown sugar, 1 tablespoon at a time, whisking well between each addition. The meringue should be glossy and holding soft peaks.

2. Spoon or pipe 18–20 golfball-sized balls of meringue onto the baking trays. Sprinkle generously with the flaked almonds and bake for 1–1¼ hours until crisp. Leave to cool on a wire rack.

3. Place the cream, rosewater and icing sugar in a large bowl and whisk until the mixture just holds soft peaks. Layer the cooled meringues, spoonfuls of cream and fruit in six tall glasses and serve immediately.

1

2

3

COOK'S NOTE
To check that the meringues are cooked, try peeling one from the lining paper. If it comes away easily, they're ready.

Baked Spicy Pudding

 SERVES 6 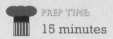 PREP TIME: 15 minutes 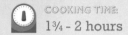 COOKING TIME: 1¾ - 2 hours

nutritional information per serving	215 kcals, 10g fat, 5g sat fat, 16g total sugars, 0.5g salt

Better known as Indian Pudding in New England. You have to try this pudding, which has withstood the passing of time, to appreciate how really good it is.

INGREDIENTS

2 tbsp raisins or sultanas

5 tbsp polenta

350 ml/12 fl oz milk

4 tbsp blackstrap molasses

2 tbsp soft dark brown sugar

½ tsp salt

30 g/1 oz butter, diced, plus extra for greasing

2 tsp ground ginger

¼ tsp cinnamon

¼ tsp ground nutmeg

2 eggs, beaten

vanilla ice cream or maple syrup, to serve

1. Preheat the oven to 150°C/300°F/Gas Mark 2. Generously grease a 850-ml/1½-pint ovenproof serving dish and set aside. Put the raisins in a sieve with 1 tablespoon of the polenta and toss well together. Shake off the excess polenta and set aside.

2. Put the milk and molasses into a saucepan over a medium–high heat and stir until the molasses is dissolved. Add the sugar and salt and continue stirring until the sugar is dissolved. Sprinkle over the remaining polenta and bring to the boil, stirring constantly. Reduce the heat and simmer for 3–5 minutes, until the mixture is thickened.

3. Remove the pan from the heat, add the butter, ginger, cinnamon and nutmeg and stir until the butter is melted. Add the eggs and beat until they are incorporated, then stir in the raisins. Pour the mixture into the prepared dish.

4. Put the dish in a small roasting tin and pour in enough boiling water to come halfway up the side of the dish. Put the dish in the preheated oven and bake, uncovered, for 1¾–2 hours, until the pudding is set and a wooden skewer inserted in the centre comes out clean.

5. Serve immediately, straight from the dish, with a dollop of ice cream on top.

Apple Fritters

 SERVES 4

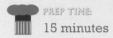 PREP TIME:
15 minutes

 COOKING TIME:
10 minutes

nutritional information per serving	434 kcals, 19.5g fat, 5g sat fat, 32g total sugars, 0.5g salt

Melting apple encased in a crisp crunchy batter and drizzled with a cinnamon glaze. Careful they're hot!

INGREDIENTS

300 g/10½ oz eating apples, such as Granny Smith, peeled, cored and cut into chunks

1 tsp lemon juice

2 eggs, separated

sunflower oil, for deep-frying and greasing

150 ml/5 fl oz milk

15 g/½ oz butter, melted

70 g/2½ oz plain white flour

70 g/2½ oz plain wholemeal flour

2 tbsp sugar

¼ tsp salt

cinnamon glaze

55 g/2 oz icing sugar

½ tsp ground cinnamon

1 tbsp milk, plus extra, if needed

1. To make the cinnamon glaze, sift the sugar and cinnamon into a small bowl and make a well in the centre. Slowly stir in the milk until smooth, then set aside.

2. Put the apples in a small bowl, add the lemon juice, toss and set aside. Beat the egg whites in a separate bowl until stiff peaks form, then set aside.

3. Heat enough oil for deep-frying in a deep-fat fryer or heavy-based saucepan until it reaches 180°C/350°F, or until a cube of bread browns in 30 seconds.

4. Meanwhile, put the egg yolks and milk into a large bowl and beat together, then stir in the butter. Sift in the white flour, wholemeal flour, sugar and salt, tipping in any bran left in the sieve, then stir the dry ingredients into the wet ingredients until just combined. Stir in the apples and their juices, then fold in the egg whites.

5. Lightly grease a spoon and use it to drop batter into the hot oil, without overcrowding the pan. Fry the fritters for 2–3 minutes, turning once, until golden brown on both sides. Transfer to kitchen paper to drain, then transfer to a wire rack. Repeat this process until all the batter is used.

6. Stir the glaze and add a little extra milk, if necessary, so that it flows freely from the tip of a spoon. Drizzle the glaze over the fritters and leave to stand for 3–5 minutes to firm up. Serve immediately.

Sweet Peach Delight

 SERVES 4   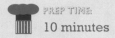 PREP TIME: 10 minutes   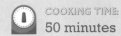 COOKING TIME: 50 minutes

nutritional information per serving	400 kcals, 14g fat, 8g sat fat, 43g total sugars, 0.6g salt

If it's a quick to prepare, fruity pudding you're after, this is just the one.

INGREDIENTS

60 g/2¼ oz butter

125 g/4½ oz wholemeal self-raising flour

175 ml/6 fl oz semi-skimmed or skimmed milk

125 g/4½ oz sugar

4 large ripe peaches, stoned, peeled and sliced

1. Preheat the oven to 180°C/350°F/Gas Mark 4. Melt the butter in a saucepan over a low heat and pour it into the base of a shallow 20-cm/8-inch square ovenproof dish.

2. Blend together the flour, milk and sugar and pour the mixture into the dish. Spoon the peach slices over the batter but do not stir. Bake in the preheated oven for 50 minutes. Serve immediately.

COOK'S TIP
You can use other seasonal fruit for this dish, such as plums or pears. You could also use good-quality, drained canned fruits.

Strawberry & Cream Whoopie Pies

 MAKES 12   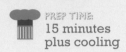 PREP TIME: 15 minutes plus cooling    COOKING TIME: 20–24 minutes

nutritional information per pie	363 kcals, 22g fat, 14g sat fat, 23g total sugars, 0.6g salt

What's a Whoopie Pie? Well it's a cross between a soft biscuit, a cake and a pie! Try this recipe and find out for yourself.

INGREDIENTS

250 g/9 oz plain flour
1 tsp bicarbonate of soda
large pinch of salt
115 g/4 oz butter, softened
150 g/5½ oz caster sugar
1 large egg, beaten
2 tsp rosewater
150 ml/5 fl oz buttermilk
icing sugar, to dust

filling

300 ml/10 fl oz double cream
4 tbsp icing sugar, sifted
3 tbsp strawberry conserve
225 g/8 oz strawberries, hulled and sliced

1. Preheat the oven to 180°C/350°F/Gas Mark 4. Line 2–3 large baking sheets with baking paper. Sift together the plain flour, bicarbonate of soda and salt.

2. Place the butter and sugar in a large bowl and beat with an electric whisk until pale and fluffy. Beat in the egg and rosewater followed by half the flour mixture and then the buttermilk. Stir in the rest of the flour mixture and mix until thoroughly incorporated.

3. Pipe or spoon 24 mounds of the mixture onto the prepared baking sheets, spaced well apart to allow for spreading. Bake in the preheated oven, one sheet at a time, for 10–12 minutes until risen and just firm to the touch. Cool for 5 minutes then using a palette knife transfer to a wire rack and leave to cool completely.

4. For the filling, place the cream in a bowl and whip until holding firm peaks. Fold in the sifted icing sugar.

5. To assemble, spread the strawberry conserve on the flat side of half of the cakes followed by the whipped cream and strawberries. Top with the rest of the cakes. Dust with icing sugar.

1

2

5

Apple Pie Pizza

 MAKES
2 pizzas

 PREP TIME:
20 minutes
plus rising

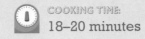 COOKING TIME:
18–20 minutes

nutritional information per pizza	1146 kcals, 28g fat, 13g sat fat, 100g total sugars, 3.9g salt

If you can't imagine a sweet pizza, then try this and you'll be hooked.

INGREDIENTS

basic pizza dough
300 g/10½ oz strong white flour, plus extra for dusting

1 tsp easy-blend dried yeast

1½ tsp salt

175 ml/6 fl oz hand-hot water

1 tbsp olive oil, plus extra for kneading

topping
3 tbsp butter

100 g/3½ oz soft light brown sugar

3 large eating apples, peeled, cored and thickly sliced

50 g/1¾ oz raisins

pinch of ground cloves

icing sugar, for dusting

1. Sift the flour into a mixing bowl and add the yeast and salt, making a small well in the top. Mix the water and oil together and pour into the bowl, using a round-bladed knife to gradually combine all the flour to make a sticky dough.

2. Lightly flour the work surface and your hands and knead the dough for about 10 minutes, until it is smooth and elastic. Cover the dough with some lightly oiled clingfilm or a damp tea towel and leave to rise for about an hour, or until it has doubled in size.

3. Knock back the dough by gently kneading for about a minute, then divide into two balls. To roll out the dough, flatten each ball, then, using a rolling pin, roll out on a lightly floured work surface, giving a quarter turn between each roll.

4. Preheat the oven to 230°C/450°F/Gas Mark 8. Place the pizza bases on two baking trays, using a rolling pin to transfer them from the work surface.

5. Melt the butter in a heavy-based non-stick frying pan over a medium heat. Add the sugar, stirring well to dissolve. Leave to bubble for 5–6 minutes, until dark and syrupy. Add the apples, raisins and cloves and cook for a further 4–5 minutes, until the apples are starting to soften but are not completely cooked.

6. Using a slotted spoon divide the apple and raisin mixture between the two pizza bases. Spoon over about half the syrup, reserving the remainder.

7. Bake in the preheated oven for 8–10 minutes, or until the bases are crisp underneath. Drizzle over the reserved syrup, dust with icing sugar and serve warm.

Apple & Lime Sorbet

 SERVES 4   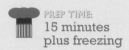 PREP TIME: 15 minutes plus freezing   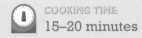 COOKING TIME: 15–20 minutes

nutritional information per serving	227 kcals, 0g fat, 0g sat fat, 56g total sugars, trace salt

An elegant dessert, yet economical too, especially if you have an apple tree in the garden!

INGREDIENTS

450 g/1 lb crisp dessert apples such as Granny Smith, Cox or Pink Lady, peeled, cored and thinly sliced

600 ml/1 pint water, plus 3 tbsp

175 g/6 oz caster sugar

finely grated zest and juice of 1 large lime

1 large egg white, lightly beaten

4 tbsp gin (optional)

slices of lime, to decorate

1. Place the apples and the 3 tablespoons of water in a saucepan. Cover and cook over a low heat for 10–15 minutes until tender. Leave to cool slightly. Transfer to a food processor and blend until completely smooth.

2. Place the sugar and remaining water in a clean saucepan and heat gently, stirring until the sugar has dissolved. Bring to the boil, then boil gently for 5 minutes. Remove from the heat. Stir in the apple and the lime zest and juice.

3. Leave for about 1 hour or until completely cool, then transfer to a freezerproof container, cover and freeze for 2–3 hours until frozen but still a little slushy in the middle.

4. Working quickly, break the frozen apple mixture into chunks and transfer to a food processor. Blend until smooth, then gradually add the egg white down the feed tube with the motor running. Continue blending for a few seconds until the sorbet looks pale and snowy. Return to the container and freeze for a further 2–3 hours until firm.

5. Serve scooped into chilled glasses, with a little gin poured over the top, if using, and decorate with slices of lime.

Rhubarb Shortcake Crumble

 SERVES 4

 PREP TIME:
15 minutes

 COOKING TIME:
45–47 minutes

nutritional information per serving | 541 kcals, 24g fat, 15g sat fat, 47g total sugars, 0.9g salt

A hybrid of one of the nation's favourite comfort foods and a moreish buttery cookie topping – what's not to like?

INGREDIENTS

600 g/1 lb 5 oz rhubarb, trimmed and cut into 4-cm/1½-in pieces

125 g/4½ oz soft light brown sugar, plus extra to taste

½ tsp ground cinnamon

zest of 1 small orange

3 tbsp water

175 g/6 oz self-raising flour

55 g/2 oz caster sugar

115 g/4 oz butter, at room temperature

custard or vanilla ice cream, to serve

1. Place the rhubarb, brown sugar, cinnamon, orange zest and water in a saucepan. Cover and cook over a very low heat for 5–7 minutes until the rhubarb is just tender and still holding its shape. Remove from the heat and add a little extra sugar to taste.

2. Preheat the oven to 160°C/325°F/Gas Mark 3. Spoon the rhubarb into an ovenproof dish.

3. Mix the flour and caster sugar together in a bowl. Add the butter in pieces and rub in with your fingertips until the mixture sticks together in small lumps.

4. Sprinkle the crumble mixture evenly over the rhubarb and bake for 40 minutes until pale golden around the edges. Serve warm with custard.

1

2

3

Garlic & Sage Bread *268*

Walnut & Seed Bread *270*

Pesto & Olive Soda Bread *272*

Plaited Poppy Seed Bread *274*

Feta & Olive Scones *276*

Cherry Tomato, Rosemary & Sea Salt Focaccia *278*

Date & Walnut Loaf *280*

Banana & Coconut Loaf *282*

Lemon Polenta Cake *284*

Carrot Cake *286*

Rich Chocolate Cake *288*

Apple & Spice Cake *290*

Espresso & Walnut Brownies *292*

Oat Bars *294*

Blueberry Granola Bars *296*

Nectarine & Banana Muffins *298*

Low-Fat Banana & Date Muffins *300*

Polenta Muffins with Chilli & Rosemary *302*

Herb Muffins with Smoked Cheese *304*

Choc Chip Muffins *306*

Chocolate & Brazil Nut Crunchies *308*

Blueberry & Passionfruit Drizzle Squares *310*

Banana Streusel Bars *312*

Cappuccino Cupcakes *314*

Breads & Baking

Garlic & Sage Bread

 MAKES
1 loaf

 PREP TIME:
20 minutes
plus rising

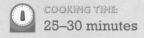 COOKING TIME:
25–30 minutes

nutritional information per loaf	841 kcals, 9g fat, 1g sat fat, 11g total sugars, 5g salt

The aroma of freshly baked bread, sage and garlic is heavenly. Don't leave to cool unattended or you may find it gone!

INGREDIENTS

250 g/9 oz strong wholemeal flour, plus extra for dusting

1 sachet easy-blend dried yeast

3 tbsp chopped fresh sage, plus fresh leaves, to garnish

1 tsp sea salt

3 garlic cloves, finely chopped

1 tsp clear honey

150 ml/5 fl oz lukewarm water

vegetable oil, for brushing

vegetarian cream cheese, to serve

1. Sift the flour into a bowl and tip in the bran from the sieve. Stir in the yeast, sage and salt. Set aside 1 teaspoon of the garlic and stir the remainder into the bowl. Make a well in the centre and pour in the honey and water. Stir well until the dough begins to come together, then knead with your hands until it leaves the side of the bowl. Turn out onto a lightly floured surface and knead for 10 minutes, or until smooth and elastic.

2. Brush a bowl with oil. Shape the dough into a ball, place it in the bowl and place the bowl into a plastic bag or cover with a damp tea towel. Leave to rise in a warm place for 1 hour, or until the dough has doubled in volume.

3. Brush a baking sheet with oil. Turn out the dough onto a lightly floured surface, and knead for 2 minutes. Roll the dough into a long sausage, shape into a ring and place it onto the baking sheet. Brush the outside of a bowl with oil and place it in the centre of the ring to prevent it from closing up while the dough is rising. Place the baking sheet into a plastic bag or cover with a damp tea towel and leave in a warm place for 30 minutes.

4. Preheat the oven to 200°C/400°F/Gas Mark 6. Remove the bowl from the centre of the loaf. Sprinkle the loaf with the reserved garlic and a little flour and bake in the preheated oven for 25–30 minutes until golden brown and the loaf sounds hollow when tapped on the base with your knuckles. Transfer to a wire rack to cool. Cut into slices, spread with cream cheese, garnish with sage leaves and serve.

Walnut & Seed Bread

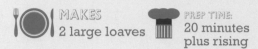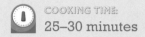

MAKES
2 large loaves

PREP TIME:
20 minutes
plus rising

COOKING TIME:
25–30 minutes

nutritional information per loaf	2200 kcals, 88g fat, 14.5g sat fat, 9g total sugars, 5.2g salt

A perfect loaf to serve with cheese and pickles. Freeze the second loaf if you don't need two.

INGREDIENTS

450 g/1 lb wholemeal flour

450 g/1 lb strong white flour, plus extra for dusting

2 tbsp sesame seeds

2 tbsp sunflower seeds

2 tbsp poppy seeds

115 g/4 oz walnuts, chopped

2 tsp salt

15 g/½ oz easy-blend dried yeast

2 tbsp olive oil or walnut oil

750 ml/1¼ pints lukewarm water

1 tbsp melted butter or oil, for greasing

1. Mix the flours, seeds, walnuts, salt and yeast together in a large bowl. Add the oil and water and stir well to form a soft dough. Turn out the dough onto a lightly floured surface and knead well for 5–7 minutes, or until smooth and elastic.

2. Return the dough to the bowl, and place the bowl in a plastic bag or cover with a damp tea towel, and leave in a warm place for 1–1½ hours to rise, or until the dough has doubled in size. Turn the dough out onto a lightly floured surface and knead again for 1 minute.

3. Grease 2 x 900-g/2-lb loaf tins well with melted butter. Divide the dough in half. Shape one piece the length of the tin and three times the width. Fold the dough in three lengthwise and place in one of the pans with the join underneath. Repeat with the other piece of dough.

4. Cover and let rise again in a warm place for about 30 minutes, or until the bread is well risen above the tins.

5. Meanwhile, preheat the oven to 230°C/450°F/Gas Mark 8. Bake in the centre of the preheated oven for 25–30 minutes, until golden brown and the loaves sound hollow when tapped on the bases with your knuckles. If the loaves are getting too brown during cooking, reduce the temperature to 220°C/425°F/Gas Mark 7. Transfer to a wire rack to cool.

Pesto & Olive Soda Bread

 MAKES
1 loaf

 PREP TIME:
15 minutes

 COOKING TIME:
30–35 minutes

nutritional information per loaf	2156 kcals, 43g fat, 4g sat fat, 21g total sugars, 6.7g salt

If you're not confident about baking with yeast try this recipe. You'll be delighted with the result. Use one of the many ready-made pestos available in shops or make your own. Either way you will have a loaf to be proud of.

INGREDIENTS

olive oil, for greasing
250 g/9 oz plain flour
250 g/9 oz wholemeal flour
1 tsp bicarbonate of soda
½ tsp salt
3 tbsp pesto
300 ml/10 fl oz buttermilk, (approx)
55 g/2 oz pitted green olives, roughly chopped
milk, for glazing

1. Preheat the oven to 200°C/400°F/Gas Mark 6 and line and grease a baking tray. Sift the flours, bicarbonate of soda and salt into a bowl, adding back any bran from the sieve.

2. Mix the pesto and buttermilk. Stir into the flour with the olives, mixing to a soft dough. Add more liquid if needed.

3. Shape the dough into a 20-cm/8-inch round and place on the baking tray. Flatten slightly and cut a deep cross with a sharp knife.

4. Brush with milk and bake in the preheated oven for 30–35 minutes, until golden brown. The loaf should sound hollow when tapped underneath. Transfer to a wire rack to cool.

1

2

3

Plaited Poppy Seed Bread

MAKES
1 loaf

PREP TIME:
20 minutes
plus rising

COOKING TIME:
30–35 minutes

nutritional information per loaf	1342 kcals, 85g fat, 14g sat fat, 56g total sugars, 4.6g salt

Ring the changes with this recipe and use other seeds such as sesame, onion or pumpkin instead of poppy.

INGREDIENTS

225 g/8 oz strong white flour, plus extra for dusting

1 tsp salt

2 tbsp skimmed milk powder

1½ tbsp caster sugar

1 tsp easy-blend dried yeast

175 ml/6 fl oz lukewarm water

2 tbsp vegetable oil, plus extra for greasing

5 tbsp poppy seeds

topping

1 egg yolk

1 tbsp milk

1 tbsp caster sugar

2 tbsp poppy seeds

1. Sift the flour and salt together into a bowl and stir in the milk powder, sugar and yeast. Make a well in the centre, pour in the water and oil and stir until the dough begins to come together. Add the poppy seeds and knead until fully combined and the dough leaves the side of the bowl. Turn out onto a lightly floured surface and knead well for about 10 minutes, until smooth and elastic.

2. Brush a bowl with oil. Shape the dough into a ball, put it in the bowl, and place the bowl in a plastic bag or cover with a damp tea towel and leave to rise in a warm place for 1 hour, or until doubled in volume.

3. Oil a baking sheet. Turn out the dough onto a lightly floured surface, and knead for 1–2 minutes. Divide into three equal pieces and shape each into a rope 25–30 cm/10–12 inches long. Place the ropes side by side and press together at one end. Plait the dough, pinch the other end together and tuck underneath.

4. Put the loaf on the prepared baking sheet, cover and leave to rise in a warm place for 30 minutes. Meanwhile, preheat the oven to 200°C/400°F/Gas Mark 6.

5. For the topping, beat the egg yolk with the milk and sugar. Brush the egg glaze over the top of the loaf and sprinkle with the poppy seeds. Bake in the preheated oven for 30–35 minutes, until golden brown. Transfer to a wire rack and leave to cool.

3

3

5

Feta & Olive Scones

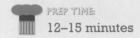 MAKES
8 scones

 PREP TIME:
12–15 minutes

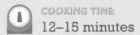 COOKING TIME:
12–15 minutes

nutritional information per scone	316 kcals, 15g fat, 8g sat fat, 2g total sugars, 1.3g salt

These would be a hit for a brunch gathering arranged in a napkin-lined basket. Serve with unsalted butter as the olives and cheese are already salty.

INGREDIENTS

400 g/14 oz self-raising flour

¼ tsp salt

85 g/3 oz butter, plus extra for greasing

40 g/1½ oz pitted black olives, chopped

40 g/1½ oz sun-dried tomatoes in oil, drained and chopped

85 g/3 oz vegetarian feta cheese (drained weight), crumbled

200 ml/7 fl oz milk, plus extra for glazing

pepper

1. Preheat the oven to 220°C/425°F/Gas Mark 7. Grease a baking sheet.

2. Sift the flour and salt, and pepper to taste, into a bowl and rub in the butter evenly with your fingers.

3. Stir in the olives, tomatoes and feta, then stir in just enough milk to make a soft, smooth dough.

4. Roll out on a floured surface to a 3-cm/1¼-inch thick rectangle. Cut into 6-cm/2½-inch squares. Place on the baking sheet, brush with milk and bake in the preheated oven for 12–15 minutes, until golden.

5. Serve the scones fresh and warm, with extra butter if needed.

2

3

4

BE PREPARED
Make the day
before and, when
cool, store in
zippered bags.
Reheat in a
moderate-high
oven for
5-10 minutes
before serving.

Cherry Tomato, Rosemary & Sea Salt Focaccia

 MAKES
1 loaf

 PREP TIME:
20 minutes
plus rising

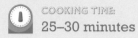 COOKING TIME:
25–30 minutes

nutritional information
per loaf

1742 kcals, 60g fat, 9g sat fat, 16g total sugars, 11g salt

A simplified version of the classic loaf studded with roasted cherry tomatoes and aromatic rosemary.

INGREDIENTS

5 tbsp olive oil

2 garlic cloves, crushed

350 g/12 oz strong white flour, plus extra for kneading

1 sachet easy-blend dried yeast

2 tsp table salt

1 tsp caster sugar

225 ml/8 fl oz lukewarm water

2 tsp finely chopped fresh rosemary

200–225g/7–8 oz ripe red cherry tomatoes

¼ tsp flaky sea salt

1. Mix 2 tablespoons of the oil and all of the garlic. Set aside. Mix the flour, yeast, table salt and sugar together in a large bowl. Add the remaining oil and water. Mix to a dough. Turn out onto a lightly floured surface and knead for 10 minutes until smooth and elastic, then knead in 1 tablespoon of the garlic-flavoured oil.

2. Oil a rectangular baking tin measuring approximately 17 x 25 cm /6½ x10 inches and at least 4 cm/1½ inches deep. Press the dough over the base of the tin with your hands. Brush with the remaining garlic oil, then scatter over the rosemary. Cover loosely with clingfilm and set aside in a warm place for about 1 hour until puffed up and doubled in size.

3. Preheat the oven to 230°C/450°F/Gas Mark 8. Scatter the tomatoes over the focaccia (squeeze in as many as you can) and press them into the base of the dough. Sprinkle with the sea salt. Place in the preheated oven and immediately reduce the temperature to 200°C/400°F/Gas Mark 6. Bake for 25–30 minutes until golden brown and the centre sounds hollow when tapped. Turn out onto a wire rack to cool. Serve warm or cold.

1

2

3

COOK'S NOTE
If you don't have a deep baking tin, press out the dough to roughly the same size on an oiled baking tray.

Date & Walnut Loaf

 MAKES
1 loaf

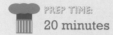 PREP TIME:
20 minutes

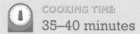 COOKING TIME:
35–40 minutes

| nutritional information per loaf | 1534 kcals, 63g fat, 28g sat fat, 134g total sugars, 2.8g salt |

This is a cross between cake and tea bread so feel free to spread slices with butter if you wish.

INGREDIENTS

100 g/3½ oz dates, stoned and chopped

½ tsp bicarbonate of soda

finely grated rind of ½ lemon

100 ml/3½ fl oz hot tea

40 g/1½ oz unsalted butter, plus extra for greasing

70 g/2½ oz light muscovado sugar

1 small egg

125 g/4½ oz self-raising flour

25 g/1 oz walnuts, chopped

walnut halves, to decorate

1. Preheat the oven to 180°C/350°F/Gas Mark 4. Grease a 450-g/1-lb loaf tin and line with baking paper.

2. Place the dates, bicarbonate of soda and lemon rind in a bowl and add the hot tea. Leave to soak for 10 minutes until softened.

3. Cream the butter and sugar together until light and fluffy, then beat in the egg. Stir in the date mixture.

4. Fold in the flour using a large metal spoon, then fold in the walnuts. Spoon the mixture into the prepared cake tin and smooth the surface. Top with the walnut halves.

5. Bake in the preheated oven for 35–40 minutes or until risen, firm and golden brown. Cool for 10 minutes in the tin, then turn out onto a wire rack to cool completely.

2

3

4

FREEZING TIP
Great for picnics and packed lunches. You can wrap slices of the cooled loaf in clingfilm and freeze for up to 3 months.

Banana & Coconut Loaf

  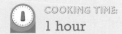

MAKES	PREP TIME:	COOKING TIME:
1 loaf	15 minutes	1 hour

nutritional information per loaf	3259 kcals, 149g fat, 58g sat fat, 251g total sugars, 2.4g salt

Over-ripe bananas can be frozen unpeeled until you're ready to make this loaf.

INGREDIENTS

250 g/9 oz plain flour

1½ tsp baking powder

200 g/7 oz caster sugar

55 g/2 oz desiccated coconut

2 eggs

90 ml/3 fl oz sunflower oil, plus extra for greasing

2 ripe bananas, mashed

125 ml/4 fl oz soured cream

1 tsp vanilla extract

long shreds of coconut, toasted, to decorate

1. Preheat the oven to 180°C/350°F/Gas Mark 4. Grease and line a 1-litre/1¾ pint loaf tin.

2. Sift together the flour and baking powder in a large bowl. Stir in the sugar and coconut. Beat together the eggs, oil, bananas, cream and vanilla extract in a large bowl. Stir into the dry ingredients, mixing until evenly combined.

3. Spoon into the prepared tin, levelling with a palette knife. Bake in the preheated oven for about 1 hour or until risen, firm and golden brown.

4. Cool in the tin for 15 minutes, then turn out onto a wire rack to cool completely. Decorate with shreds of coconut and serve.

Lemon Polenta Cake

 SERVES 8    PREP TIME: 20 minutes plus cooling    COOKING TIME: 30–35 minutes

nutritional information **per serving**   503 kcals, 34g fat, 15g sat fat, 33g total sugars, 0.24g salt

Polenta is the Italian name for cornmeal and provides a nutty texture to a lemon syrup soaked cake.

INGREDIENTS

200 g/7 oz unsalted butter, plus extra for greasing

200 g/7 oz caster sugar

finely grated rind and juice of 1 large lemon

3 eggs, beaten

140 g/5 oz ground almonds

100 g/3½ oz quick-cook polenta

1 tsp baking powder

crème fraîche, to serve

syrup

juice of 2 lemons

55 g/2 oz caster sugar

2 tbsp water

1. Preheat the oven to 180°C/350°F/Gas Mark 4. Grease a 20-cm/8-inch deep round cake tin and line with baking paper.

2. Beat together the butter and sugar until pale and fluffy. Beat in the lemon rind, lemon juice, eggs and ground almonds. Sift in the polenta and baking powder and stir until evenly mixed. Spoon the mixture into the prepared tin and smooth the surface. Bake in the preheated oven for 30–35 minutes, or until just firm to the touch and golden brown. Remove the cake from the oven and leave to cool in the tin for 20 minutes.

3. To make the syrup, place the lemon juice, sugar and water in a small saucepan. Heat gently, stirring until the sugar has dissolved, then bring to the boil and simmer for 3–4 minutes, or until slightly reduced and syrupy. Turn out the cake onto a wire rack then brush half of the syrup evenly over the surface. Leave to cool completely.

4. Cut the cake into slices, drizzle the extra syrup over the top and serve with crème fraîche.

SOMETHING
DIFFERENT
Use orange rind
and juice in place
of the lemon and
serve the cake as
a special dessert
accompanied by
caramel soaked
oranges.

Carrot Cake

 MAKES
6 bars

 PREP TIME:
20 minutes
plus cooling

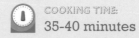 COOKING TIME:
35-40 minutes

nutritional information per bar	493 kcals, 24g fat, 8g sat fat, 54g total sugars, 0.6g salt

It's amazing that grated carrot incorporated into a cake recipe can taste so delicious. Maybe it's the cream cheese icing on the top!

INGREDIENTS

butter, for greasing
100 g/3½ oz self-raising flour
pinch of salt
1 tsp ground mixed spice
½ tsp ground nutmeg
125 g/4½ oz soft light brown sugar
2 eggs, beaten
5 tbsp sunflower oil
125 g/4½ oz carrots, grated
1 banana, chopped
25 g/1 oz chopped toasted mixed nuts

icing

40 g/1½ oz butter, softened
3 tbsp vegetarian cream cheese
175 g/6 oz icing sugar, sifted
1 tsp fresh orange juice
grated rind of ½ orange
walnut halves or pieces, to decorate

1. Preheat the oven to 180°C/350°F/Gas Mark 4. Grease an 18-cm/7-inch square cake tin and line with baking paper.

2. Sift the flour, salt, mixed spice and nutmeg into a bowl. Stir in the brown sugar, then stir in the eggs and oil. Add the carrots, banana and nuts and mix well together.

3. Spoon the mixture into the prepared tin and level the surface. Bake in the preheated oven for 35-40 minutes, or until golden and just firm to the touch. Leave to cool slightly. When cool enough to handle, turn out onto a wire rack and leave to cool completely.

4. To make the icing, put the butter, cream cheese, icing sugar and orange juice and rind in a bowl and beat together until creamy. Spread the icing over the top of the cold cake, then use a fork to make shallow, wavy lines in the icing. Scatter over the walnuts, cut the cake into bars and serve.

Rich Chocolate Cake

 SERVES 12

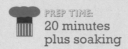 PREP TIME:
20 minutes
plus soaking

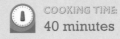 COOKING TIME:
40 minutes

nutritional information per serving	312 kcals, 22g fat, 10g sat fat, 19g total sugars, 0.5g salt

A cake for adults who appreciate the intense flavour of a good quality chocolate. No need for icing – just a light sprinkling of icing sugar. Enjoy.

INGREDIENTS

100 g/3½ oz raisins

finely grated rind and juice of 1 orange

175 g/6 oz butter, diced, plus extra for greasing

100 g/3½ oz plain chocolate, at least 70 per cent cocoa solids, broken into pieces

4 large eggs, beaten

100 g/3½ oz caster sugar

1 tsp vanilla essence

55 g/2 oz plain flour

55 g/2 oz ground almonds

½ tsp baking powder

pinch of salt

55 g/2 oz blanched almonds, lightly toasted and chopped

icing sugar, sifted, to decorate

1. Preheat the oven to 180°C/350°F/Gas Mark 4. Line a deep, loose-based, 25-cm/10-inch round cake tin with greaseproof paper. Grease the paper.

2. Put the raisins in a small bowl, add the orange juice and leave to soak for 20 minutes.

3. Melt the butter and chocolate together in a small saucepan over a medium heat, stirring. Remove from the heat and set aside to cool.

4. Using an electric mixer, beat the eggs, sugar and vanilla essence together for 3 minutes, or until light and fluffy. Stir in the cooled chocolate mixture.

5. Drain the raisins if they have not absorbed all the orange juice. Sift the flour, ground almonds, baking powder and salt into the egg and sugar mixture. Add the raisins, orange rind and almonds and fold all the ingredients together.

6. Spoon into the cake tin and smooth the surface. Bake in the preheated oven for 40 minutes, or until a cocktail stick inserted into the centre comes out clean and the cake starts to come away from the side of the tin. Leave to cool in the tin for 10 minutes, then remove from the tin, transfer to a wire rack and leave to cool completely. Dust the surface with icing sugar before serving.

Espresso & Walnut Brownies

 MAKES 9    PREP TIME: 20 minutes plus cooling   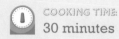 COOKING TIME: 30 minutes

nutritional information
per brownie   400 kcals, 24g fat, 11g sat fat, 28g total sugars, 0.45g salt

Some people spend their whole life searching for the perfect brownie. You need go no further.

INGREDIENTS

115 g/4 oz butter, plus extra for greasing

175 g/6 oz plain chocolate, roughly chopped

175 g/6 oz self-raising flour

2 tbsp instant espresso coffee powder

75 g/2¾ oz walnut pieces, chopped

2 eggs, beaten

150 g/5½ oz light muscovado sugar

1. Preheat the oven to 180°C/350°F/Gas Mark 4. Grease and line an 18-cm/7-inch square cake tin with baking paper.

2. Put the butter and 55 g/2 oz of the chocolate in a heatproof bowl. Place the bowl over a pan of simmering water and heat until the butter and chocolate have just melted. Remove from the heat and allow to cool for 10 minutes.

3. Mix together the flour, coffee powder, remaining chocolate and chopped walnuts in a large bowl. Place the eggs and sugar in another bowl and beat with a wooden spoon for a few minutes to break down any lumps of sugar. Add the cooled chocolate mixture, then the flour mixture and beat until thoroughly combined.

4. Transfer the mixture to the prepared tin and place in the centre of the preheated oven. Bake for 30 minutes until the mixture is set, crusted over and cracked but still a little gooey in the centre. Allow to cool in the tin before cutting into nine pieces and serving.

COOK'S NOTE

To prevent the chocolate from flying about when you chop it, have a tall jug of hot water and a clean cloth to hand. Warm the knife in the water, wipe dry and the job will be a lot easier.

Oat Bars

 MAKES 16   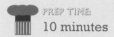 PREP TIME: 10 minutes    COOKING TIME: 20 minutes

nutritional information per bar	250 kcals, 16g fat, 7g sat fat, 13g total sugars, trace salt

Going on a long journey? You'll be really pleased you took a batch of these with you to keep you going, and so will everyone else you meet.

INGREDIENTS

175 g/6 oz unsalted butter, plus extra for greasing

3 tbsp clear honey

150 g/5½ oz demerara sugar

100 g/3½ oz smooth peanut butter

225 g/8 oz rolled oats

50 g/1¾ oz chopped ready-to-eat dried apricots

2 tbsp sunflower seeds

2 tbsp sesame seeds

1. Preheat the oven to 180°C/350°F/Gas Mark 4. Grease and line a 22-cm/8½-inch square baking tin.

2. Melt the butter, honey and sugar in a saucepan over a low heat. When the sugar has melted, add the peanut butter and stir until everything is well combined. Add all the remaining ingredients and mix well.

3. Press the mixture into the prepared tin and bake in the preheated oven for 20 minutes. Remove from the oven and leave to cool in the tin, then cut into 16 squares and serve.

COOK'S NOTE
Use non-stick baking paper to line your tin as it's easier than ordinary greaseproof paper.

Blueberry Granola Bars

 MAKES 12

 PREP TIME:
10 minutes

 COOKING TIME:
20 minutes

nutritional information per bar	270 kcals, 15g fat, 6g sat fat, 11g total sugars, 0.2g salt

Great for packed lunches, these will keep for up to a week in an airtight tin – if they last that long!

INGREDIENTS

115 g/4 oz dried blueberries
225 g/8 oz rolled oats
40 g/1½ oz soft light brown sugar
50 g/1¾ oz pecan nuts, chopped
25 g/1 oz sunflower seeds
1 tbsp sesame seeds
¼ tsp ground cinnamon
115 g/4 oz golden syrup
115 g/4 oz butter, plus extra for greasing

1. Preheat the oven to 180°C/350°F/Gas Mark 4. Grease and line 18 x 28-cm/7 x 11-inch baking tin.

2. Put the blueberries, oats, sugar, pecan nuts, seeds and cinnamon into a large bowl.

3. Heat the golden syrup and butter in a pan over a low heat until just melted. Stir in the dry ingredients to coat thoroughly. Transfer the mixture to the prepared tin and smooth the surface.

4. Place in the preheated oven and bake for 20 minutes until golden. Remove from the oven and leave to cool for 5 minutes before marking into 12 bars.

5. Allow to cool completely in the tin and then cut through the markings to create 12 bars.

SOMETHING
DIFFERENT
If you can't
find dried
blueberries,
experiment with
other dried
fruits such as
cranberries,
cherries and
strawberries.

Low-Fat Banana & Date Muffins

 MAKES 12

 PREP TIME:
15 minutes

 COOKING TIME:
20–25 minutes

nutritional information per muffin	142 kcals, 0.7g fat, 0.3g sat fat, 18g total sugars, 0.3g salt

Adding banana to this low-fat recipe is the secret to creating a moist muffin.

INGREDIENTS

oil or melted butter, for greasing (if using)

215 g/7½ oz plain flour

2 tsp baking powder

¼ tsp salt

½ tsp ground mixed spice

5 tbsp caster sugar

2 egg whites

2 ripe bananas, sliced

75 g/2¾ oz ready-to-eat dried dates, stoned and chopped

4 tbsp skimmed milk

5 tbsp maple syrup

1. Preheat the oven to 200°C/400°F/Gas Mark 6. Grease a 12-cup muffin tin or line with 12 paper cases.

2. Sift together the flour, baking powder, salt and mixed spice into a large bowl. Add the sugar and mix together.

3. In a separate large bowl, whisk the egg whites. Mash the bananas in another bowl, then add them to the egg whites. Add the dates, then pour in the milk and maple syrup and stir together gently to mix. Make a well in the centre of the dry ingredients and pour in the liquid ingredients. Stir gently until just combined; do not over-mix.

4. Spoon the mixture into the prepared muffin tin. Bake in the preheated oven for 20–25 minutes, until well risen, golden brown and firm to the touch.

5. Leave the muffins in the tin for 5 minutes, then serve warm or transfer to a wire rack and leave to cool.

3

3

4

SOMETHING
DIFFERENT
Dried figs
would be a great
alternative to the
dates but use
plump juicy ones
that don't require
soaking.

Herb Muffins with Smoked Cheese

 MAKES 12

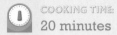 PREP TIME: 15 minutes

 COOKING TIME: 20 minutes

nutritional information per muffin	154 kcals, 6.5g fat, 4g sat fat, 2g total sugars, 0.5g salt

The secret of a good muffin is not to over-stir the batter. Gently fold the liquid and dry ingredients together.

INGREDIENTS

oil or melted butter, for greasing (if using)

280 g/10 oz plain flour

2 tsp baking powder

½ tsp bicarbonate of soda

25 g/1 oz smoked vegetarian hard cheese, grated

50 g/1¾ oz fresh parsley, finely chopped

1 egg

300 ml/10 fl oz thick natural yogurt

55 g/2 oz butter, melted and cooled

1. Preheat the oven to 200°C/400°F/Gas Mark 6. Grease a 12-cup muffin tin or line with 12 paper cases.

2. Sift together the flour, baking powder and bicarbonate of soda into a large bowl. Stir in the cheese and parsley.

3. Lightly beat the egg in a large jug, then beat in the yogurt and melted butter. Make a well in the centre of the dry ingredients and pour in the beaten liquid ingredients. Stir gently until just combined; do not over-mix.

4. Spoon the mixture into the prepared muffin tin. Bake in the preheated oven for 20 minutes, until well risen, golden brown and firm to the touch.

5. Leave the muffins in the tin for 5 minutes, then serve warm or transfer to a wire rack and leave to cool.

COOK'S NOTE

Always allow muffins to cool for at least 5 minutes in the tin before transferring to a wire rack. Sometimes, the steam from the muffins can cause the paper case to pull away if turned out too soon.

Choc Chip Muffins

 MAKES 12

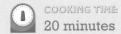 PREP TIME: 15 minutes

 COOKING TIME: 20 minutes

nutritional information per muffin — 215 kcals, 8g fat, 5g sat fat, 14g total sugars, 0.4g salt

Everyone's favourite muffin which will stand on its own in a contest with cookies and cupcakes.

INGREDIENTS

250 g/9 oz wholemeal self-raising flour

4 tbsp cocoa powder

70 g/2½ oz soft light brown sugar

100 g/3½ oz milk or plain chocolate chips

175 ml/6 fl oz reduced-fat Greek-style yogurt

200 ml/7 fl oz semi-skimmed milk

1 large egg

1 large ripe banana

50 g/1¾ oz butter

1. Preheat the oven to 200°C/400°F/Gas Mark 6 and line a 12-cup muffin tin with paper cases. Sift the flour and cocoa powder into a bowl and stir in the sugar and chocolate chips.

2. Beat together the yogurt, milk and egg in another bowl. Mash the banana in a dish with a fork until almost liquid. Melt the butter in a saucepan over a low heat and stir into the banana. Add the banana mixture to the yogurt mixture and stir well.

3. Add the wet ingredients to the dry mixture and stir until just blended. Divide the mixture among the muffin cases and bake in the preheated oven for 20 minutes, until risen and just firm to the touch.

4. Leave the muffins in the tin for 5 minutes, then transfer to a wire rack to cool.

1

2

3

COOK'S TIP
The muffins
will keep for
1-2 days in an
airtight container
but are best eaten
as soon as they
are cool.

Chocolate & Brazil Nut Crunchies

 MAKES 30

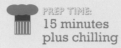 PREP TIME:
15 minutes
plus chilling

 COOKING TIME:
15 minutes

nutritional information
per cookie

123 kcals, 7g fat, 3g sat fat, 8g total sugars, 0.16g salt

A batch of these will disappear from the cookie jar in a flash.

INGREDIENTS

55 g/2 oz butter or margarine,
plus extra for greasing

55 g/2 oz white vegetable fat

140 g/5 oz demerara sugar

1 egg

1 tsp vanilla essence

1 tbsp milk

100 g/3½ oz plain flour, unsifted

100 g/3½ oz rolled oats

1 tsp bicarbonate of soda

pinch of salt

175 g/6 oz plain chocolate chips

75 g/2¾ oz Brazil nuts, chopped

1. Put the butter, fat, sugar, egg, vanilla essence and milk in a blender or food processor and process for at least 3 minutes until a fluffy consistency is reached.

2. Mix the flour, oats, bicarbonate of soda and salt together in a large bowl. Stir in the egg mixture, then the chocolate chips and nuts and mix well together. Cover the bowl with clingfilm and chill in the refrigerator for 30 minutes until firm.

3. Meanwhile, preheat the oven to 180°C/350°F/Gas Mark 4. Grease a large baking tray.

4. Put 30 rounded tablespoonfuls of the mixture onto the prepared baking tray, making sure that they are well spaced. Bake in the pre-heated oven for 15 minutes, or until golden brown.

5. Transfer to a wire rack to cool before serving.

1

2

4

FREEZING TIP
Make the dough and form into a roll. Wrap in foil and freeze for up to 3 months. Defrost until soft enough to slice then place on baking sheets and bake.

Blueberry & Passionfruit Drizzle Squares

 MAKES
9 squares

 PREP TIME:
15 minutes

 COOKING TIME:
25–30 minutes

nutritional information per square	358 kcals, 16g fat, 9g sat fat, 35g total sugars, 0.5g salt

The name alone makes your mouth water and they will not disappoint. An excellent dessert recipe served with yogurt or cream.

INGREDIENTS

150 g/5½ oz butter, softened, plus extra for greasing
2 eggs
175 g/6 oz golden caster sugar
175 g/6 oz self-raising flour, sifted
90 ml/3 fl oz milk
finely grated zest of 1 lemon
225 g/8 oz blueberries

syrup
4 ripe passionfruit
115 g/4 oz icing sugar, plus extra, sifted, for dusting

1. Preheat the oven to 190°C/375°F/Gas Mark 5. Grease and line the base of a 23-cm/9-inch square cake tin.

2. Whisk the butter, eggs and sugar until pale and fluffy. Fold in the flour lightly and evenly. Stir in the milk, lemon zest and 175 g/6 oz of the blueberries. Spread into the cake tin.

3. Bake in the preheated oven for 25–30 minutes, until firm and golden brown. Remove from the oven and leave in the tin.

4. Meanwhile, make the syrup. Scoop the pulp from the passionfruit and rub through a sieve. Discard the pips. Place the sugar and passionfruit juice in a saucepan and heat gently, stirring, until the sugar dissolves.

5. Prick the warm cake with a fork and spoon the syrup evenly over the surface. Leave the cake to cool completely in the tin, then cut into nine squares. Top the squares with the reserved blueberries and dust with icing sugar before serving.

Banana Streusel Bars

 MAKES 10

 PREP TIME:
20 minutes

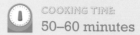 COOKING TIME:
50–60 minutes

nutritional information
per bar

438 kcals, 24g fat, 11g sat fat, 26g total sugars, 0.6g salt

This is a great way of using up a slightly too-ripe banana with dark blotches on the skin. It will give the bars much more flavour than a pristine yellow one.

INGREDIENTS

200 g/7 oz butter, plus extra for greasing

115 g/4 oz soft dark brown sugar

150 g/5½ oz jumbo porridge oats

55 g/2 oz pecan nuts, chopped

½ tsp ground cinnamon

115 g/4 oz caster sugar

2 eggs, lightly beaten

140 g/5 oz peeled ripe banana, mashed

200 g/7 oz self-raising flour

1. Preheat the oven to 180°C/350°F/Gas Mark 4. Grease an 18-cm/ 7-inch square cake tin and line with non-stick baking paper. Place 85 g/3 oz of the butter and the brown sugar in a saucepan over a low heat and stir until melted and smooth. Remove from the heat. Stir in the oats, nuts and cinnamon. Set aside.

2. Beat the remaining 115 g/4 oz of the butter and the caster sugar together until creamy, gradually add the eggs, beating well after each addition. Fold in the banana and flour with a large metal spoon.

3. Spread half the cake mixture over the base of the prepared tin. Sprinkle half the oat mixture over the top, then repeat the layers once. Bake in the preheated oven for 50–60 minutes until risen and the centre is firm to the touch. Leave to cool in tin for about 1 hour, then turn out and cut into ten bars.

1

2

3

FREEZING TIP
Put the cooked bars in a freezerproof box, placing greaseproof paper between the layers. Freeze for up to 4 months. Thaw for 1 hour at room temperature.

Index

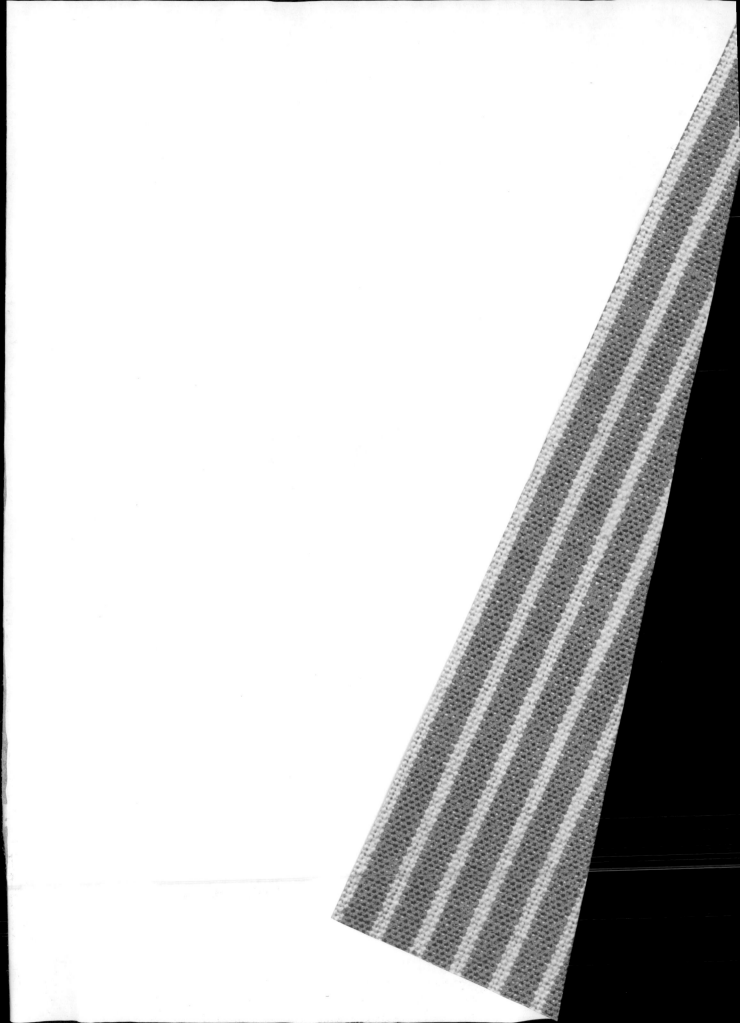